Ravenscourt

B·O·O·K·S

Teacher's Guide

Anything's Possible

Books 1-8

Adventures on the Nile
Hyperlinking through the Solar System
Seven Wonders of the World
Race to Space
Around the World
Earth Belongs to You
Treasure Island
Gulliver's Travels

McGraw Hill SRA

Columbus, OH

SRAonline.com

 SRA

Send all inquiries to this address:
SRA/McGraw-Hill
4400 Easton Commons
Columbus, OH 43219

ISBN: 978-0-07-611312-5
MHID: 0-07-611312-4

1 2 3 4 5 6 7 8 9 MAL 13 12 11 10 09 08 07

The McGraw·Hill Companies

Table of Contents

Placing Students

Written for middle school to young adult readers, **Ravenscourt Books** provides materials and activities for enhancing the comprehension and fluency of struggling readers. Each of these fiction and nonfiction selections are

- organized within themes that are both engaging and informative.

- built to provide students with additional opportunities to read independently.

- designed to provide frequent opportunities for reading to improve fluency and overall reading achievement.

Some teachers have found these selections align with the independent reading levels of students in the **Corrective Reading** program. Use the chart below to place your students in the appropriate set of **Ravenscourt Readers**.

	For students who have successfully completed	Reading level	Page count (average number of words per book)
Getting Started	Corrective Reading Decoding A*	1	32 (800)
Discovery	Corrective Reading Comprehension A*	1	32 (1,800)
Anything's Possible	Corrective Reading Decoding B1*	2	32 (1,800)
The Unexpected	Corrective Reading Comprehension B1*	2	32 (1,800)
Express Yourself	Corrective Reading Decoding B2*	3	48 (4,200)
Overcoming Adversity	Corrective Reading Comprehension B2*	3	48 (4,200)
Moving Forward	Corrective Reading Decoding C* Lesson 60	5	64 (7,500)
Reaching Goals	Corrective Reading Comprehension C* Lesson 60	5	64 (7,500)

*or have attained comparable skills

Components

The **Using *Ravenscourt Books*** section explains how to incorporate these components into an effective supplemental reading program.

Chapter Books

- Include eight age-appropriate books in each set
- Feature fiction, nonfiction, and retold classics
- Present additional practice for essential vocabulary and decoding skills
- Provide fast-moving story lines for independent reading

Fluency Audio CDs

- Model pronunciation, phrasing, intonation, and expression
- Assist students in improving their oral-reading fluency

Evaluation and Tracking Software

- Motivates students by delivering activities electronically
- Scores, records, and tracks student progress

Teacher's Guides

- Outline ways to use the series in your classroom
- Include comprehension activities, word lists, and fluency practice
- Provide prereading activities and postreading writing activities
- Address reading and language arts standards

Online Support

Go to **SRAonline.com** and click on **Ravenscourt Books** for additional support and materials.

Reading and Fluency

Reading

Reading is not simply decoding or word recognition; it is understanding the text. Students who read slowly or hesitantly are not able to concentrate on meaning.

Fluency

Fluency bridges the gap between decoding and comprehension and characterizes proficient reading. Increased oral-reading fluency improves reading comprehension.

Fluent and Nonfluent Readers

The chart below presents an easy way to compare fluent and nonfluent readers. If students have several of the listed characteristics of nonfluent readers, refer to the sections on *Assessing Fluency* and *Fluency Practice* in the **Using *Ravenscourt Books*** section that begins on page 3.

A Fluent Reader	A Nonfluent Reader
Reads words accurately	Reads with omissions, pauses, mispronunciations, insertions, and substitutions
Decodes automatically	Reverses word order
Reads smoothly	Reads word-by-word, focusing on words
Reads at an appropriate rate	Reads slowly, hesitantly
Reads with expression and phrasing	Reads without expression; ignores punctuation
Reads with understanding of text	Reads with limited comprehension
Reads so text sounds like speech	Reads without natural intonation

Oral-Reading Fluency

Oral-reading fluency is the ability to read accurately, at an appropriate rate, and with good expression and phrasing. The foundation for oral-reading fluency is automatic word recognition and extensive practice with materials that are easy for the students to read.

Oral-reading fluency develops as a result of multiple opportunities to practice reading successfully. The primary strategy for developing oral-reading fluency is to provide extensive and frequent opportunities for students to read text with high levels of accuracy. This means that selected passages should be ones the students are able to read with at least 95 percent accuracy.

Repeated and monitored oral reading is an effective intervention strategy for students who do not read fluently. By reading the same passage a number of times, students become familiar with the words it contains and recognize the words automatically. This improves reading fluency and overall reading achievement. It also builds confidence and motivation—particularly when students chart their progress.

The minimum target oral-reading fluency rate is 60 *words read correctly per minute* (wcpm) for **Getting Started** and **Discovery,** 90 wcpm for **Anything's Possible** and **The Unexpected,** 130 wcpm for **Express Yourself** and **Overcoming Adversity,** and 150 wcpm for **Moving Forward** and **Reaching Goals.**

How to assess fluency, how to set realistic target rates, and how to practice fluency will be discussed in greater detail in the **Using *Ravenscourt Books*** section.

Grouping

Students who have completed *Decoding B1* will have mastered the decoding skills and vocabulary necessary to independently read the stories in **Anything's Possible.**

Ravenscourt Books may be taught to the whole class, small groups, or pairs. Assign each student to a partner. Partners can do paired readings for fluency practice. The partners will read the same story at the same time. *Ravenscourt Books* may also be used for individual student reading.

Scheduling

Ravenscourt Books is intended to be used as a supplement to your core program and should be scheduled in addition to the regular lessons. Times to use the books include

- reading and language arts blocks,
- before- and after-school programs,
- summer school,
- and out-of-school reading with parental support.

	A Suggested Lesson Plan for *Ravenscourt Books*
Part 1	1) Introduce the series, and help students select a book. 2) Assess students' initial oral-reading fluency by completing a "cold read" of one of the book's fluency passages. The **Fluency Passage** section can be found after the **Thinking and Writing** section for each book. (See *Assessing Fluency* on page 4.) 3) Have students complete the **Building Background** activities.
Part 2	1) Preteach the unfamiliar words for the first chapter in the **Word Lists** section of the *Teacher's Guide* for each book. 2) Have students read the title of the first chapter aloud. 3) Have students listen to a fluent reader read the first chapter as they follow along with the text. 4) Have student pairs take turns reading the chapter again. 5) Have students take the **Chapter Quiz.** 6) Have some students do repeated readings to improve oral-reading fluency. 7) Repeat Part 2 for subsequent chapters.
Part 3	1) Have students complete the **Thinking and Writing** section. 2) Take fluency scores, using the same fluency passage used in Part 1. Have students enter their scores on their **Fluency Graph.**

Selecting Books

The books in each set are leveled so students can start with any book in the set. However, students generally find contemporary fiction easier to read than nonfiction and retold classics.

On pages 10–11 you will find **Book Summaries** that give a brief outline of each book.

- If the book is a retold classic, information about the original author is included.

- If the book is a good tool for teaching a literary term, the term is explained. The teacher should teach the term before the students begin reading.

- The last section includes other resources—books, films, or Web sites—that contain related information. These resources can be used for extra credit, reports, projects, and so on. Evaluate all books, films, and Web sites to confirm appropriateness of the content prior to sharing these materials with students.

Using *Ravenscourt Books*

Introducing the Series

1. Write the series theme on the board.
   - Tell the students that the books in the set all relate in some way to this common theme.
   - Brainstorm ideas about the theme, and write the students' ideas on a large sheet of chart paper. Include words, topics, and types of stories related to the theme. Post this list for student reference.

2. The books in each set represent several genres—fiction, nonfiction, biography, science fiction, historical fiction, retold classics, and so on.
   - Ask the students to read the title and the summary on the back of the book they chose.
   - Have the students predict how their book relates to the theme.
   - If the book is nonfiction, ask the student to predict what kinds of questions it could answer.

Whole-Class Instruction

The following sections are designed for whole-class instruction but may be modified for small groups or individual instruction.

Set up classes in the *Evaluation and Tracking Software,* or make a copy of the **Individual Progress Chart** for each student.

Assessing Fluency

Make a class set of copies of the **Fluency Graph** on page 9 of the *Teacher's Guide.* Follow these steps to **ASSESS STUDENTS' INITIAL ORAL-READING FLUENCY.**

1. Have the student read a passage that is set at the appropriate length (60–150 words) and at the appropriate instructional reading level (at least 95 percent accuracy).
   - The **Fluency Passage** section can be found after the **Thinking and Writing** section for each book.

2. Ask the student to do a one-minute reading of the unrehearsed passage.

3. Ask the student whether she or he is ready.
   - Then say: **Please begin.**

4. Follow along as the student reads.
   - When an error occurs, mark the error.
   - Count the following as errors: mispronunciations, omissions, substitutions, insertions, and failure to identify a word within three seconds.
   - Don't mark words the student self-corrects.
   - Don't mark off for proper nouns.

5. At the end of one minute, make a vertical line on the page after the last word read.

6. Count the number of words up to the last word read.

7. Subtract the number of errors to determine the wcpm.

8. Enter the number of words read correctly on the student's **Fluency Graph** by filling in the column to the appropriate number.

9. At the bottom of the graph, circle the number of errors made.

10. Review any words the student missed and provide practice on those words. The minimum goals for fluency are the following:
    - The goal for students who have completed *Decoding A* or have equivalent skills is to read the books in **Getting Started** at a minimum rate of 60 wcpm.
    - The goal for students who have completed *Comprehension A* or have equivalent skills is to read the books in **Discovery** at a minimum rate of 60 wcpm.
    - The goal for students who have completed *Decoding B1* or have equivalent skills is to read the books in **Anything's Possible** at a minimum rate of 90 wcpm.
    - The goal for students who have completed *Comprehension B1* or have equivalent skills is to read the books in **The Unexpected** at a minimum rate of 90 wcpm.

- The goal for students who have completed *Decoding B2* or have equivalent skills is to read the books in **Express Yourself** at a minimum rate of 130 wcpm.

- The goal for students who have completed *Comprehension B2* or have equivalent skills is to read the books in **Overcoming Adversity** at a minimum rate of 130 wcpm.

- The goal for students who have completed Lesson 60 of *Decoding C* or have equivalent skills is to read the books in **Moving Forward** at a minimum rate of 150 wcpm.

- The goal for students who have completed Lesson 60 of *Comprehension C* or have equivalent skills is to read the books in **Reaching Goals** at a minimum rate of 150 wcpm.

Word Lists

Follow this procedure to preteach the words for each chapter of every book.

1. Provide students with a copy of the **Word Lists** page, or copy the words onto the board. Underline word parts if appropriate.

2. Begin with *Proper Nouns* by saying:
   - **These are the names of important people and places in Chapter 1.**
   - **Touch the first word in the column.**
   - Point to an underlined word part (if necessary) and say: **What sound?** (Signal.)
   - **What word?** (Signal.)
   - (Repeat until firm.)

3. For difficult and irregular words, say:
   - **Touch the word.**
   - **The word is _____.** (Signal.)
   - **What word?** (Signal.)
   - **Spell _____.** (Signal for each letter.)
   - **What word?** (Signal.)
   - (Repeat until firm.)

4. Follow the same procedure with *Unfamiliar Words.* Discuss the meanings of the words. Use the words in sentences as needed. The *Word Meanings* category is comprised of the words used in the *Word Meanings* section of **Building Background,** so some of the words may be familiar. Only use the following procedure for unfamiliar words.
   - Point to each unfamiliar word, say the word, and then say **What does _____ mean?** (Call on individual students.)
   - (Repeat until firm.)

Building Background

Use the **Building Background** section in the *Teacher's Guide* or on the *Evaluation and Tracking Software.* You can use this section as a whole-class activity or as an independent activity.

Whole-Class Activity

1. Divide the students into small groups. Hand out copies of the **Building Background** page for that book.

2. Read the questions in the *What You Know* section. Have the groups discuss the questions and write an answer for them. Have a member of each group read the group's answers to the class.

3. Read the words in the *Word Meanings* section.
   - Then read the directions and go over each question with the students and say, **Which word best answers this question?** (Call on individual students.)
   - Repeat this procedure for all of the words. (Note: If the directions indicate that the questions should be answered once the words have been introduced in the book, go over each word again after the students have read the word in context and have them answer the question associated with that word.)

4. Collect the papers and score them based on the number of correct answers. Refer to the **Answer Key** for each book.

Using *Ravenscourt Books*

Independent Activity

1. Hand out copies of the **Building Background** page. Have students take turns reading each question in the *What You Know* section. Have students write their answers before proceeding to the next question.

2. Have students read the words in the *Word Meanings* section. Then have them read the directions and complete the section.

   • When students are finished, collect the papers and score them based on completion and effort. Refer to to the **Answer Key** for each book.

The teacher may enter the scores on the **Individual Progress Chart** found in the *Teacher's Guide* or on the *Evaluation and Tracking Software.*

Reading the Chapter

First, the students listen to a fluent reader read the chapter. The fluency model may be the teacher, a parent, a tutor, a teacher's aide, a peer, or the *Fluency Audio CDs.* Students read along, tracking the text with their fingers. Next, students take turns reading the chapter with their peer partner. An individual student reads aloud to the teacher, tutor, or parent, who gives feedback, points out missed words, and models, using punctuation, to improve expressive reading.

Chapter Quiz

After the second reading of the chapter, the student takes the **Chapter Quiz.** The quizzes have multiple-choice, true-or-false, sequence, and short-answer questions. The chapter quizzes are available on the *Evaluation and Tracking Software* or as blackline masters in the *Teacher's Guide.* Use the **Answer Keys** to score the blackline masters and enter scores on the **Individual Progress Chart** found on page 8. The *Evaluation and Tracking Software* will automatically grade and record the scores for all non-short-answer questions for each **Chapter Quiz.**

Students should take each quiz once and do their best the first time. Students must score a minimum of 80 percent to continue. If the student does not score 80 percent, he or she should reread the chapter before retaking the quiz.

Fluency Practice

Fluency practice improves comprehension. The teacher may choose different ways to practice fluency, depending on the student's needs. For students who are close to the target rate, have the student reread the whole chapter using one of these techniques:

   • **Echo reading** A fluent reader reads a sentence aloud, and the student *echoes* it—repeats it with the same intonation and phrasing.

   • **Unison or choral reading** A pair, group, or class reads a chapter aloud together.

   • **Paired reading** The student reads a page aloud and receives feedback from his or her peer partner. Record the fluency scores on the **Fluency Graph** found in the *Teacher's Guide* or on the *Evaluation and Tracking Software.* Recording progress motivates student achievement.

For students who are significantly below the target rate, conduct **REPEATED READINGS TO IMPROVE ORAL-READING FLUENCY.** The student will reread the passages marked by asterisks in each of the books' chapters.

1. Set a target rate for the passage.

   • The target rate should be high enough to require the student to reread the passage several times.

   • A reasonable target rate is 40 percent higher than the baseline level.

   • For example, if the student initially reads the passage at a rate of 60 wcpm, the target rate for that passage would be 84 wcpm (**60** x .40 = 24; **60** + 24 = 84).

2. Have the student listen to the passage read fluently by a skilled reader or on the corresponding *Fluency Audio CD* while following along, pointing to the words as they are read.

3. After listening to the fluency model, have the student reread the same passage aloud for one minute.

   • A partner listens and records errors but does not interrupt the reader during the one-minute timed reading.

   • If the student makes more than six errors, he or she should listen to the fluency model again.

4. The student should read the same passage three to five times during the session or until the target rate is met, whichever comes first.

   • After each rereading, the student records the wcpm on his or her **Fluency Graph.**

   • If the target rate is not met, have the student read the same passage again the next day.

   • If the target rate is met, the student repeats the procedure with the next chapter.

Thinking and Writing

Many state assessments require students to produce extended writing about a story or an article they have read. Like **Building Background,** this section is not computer-scored and may be used in one of several ways. The *Think About It* section is intended to help students summarize what they have read and to relate the book to other books in the set, to the theme, or to the students' life experiences.

1. The questions in the *Think About It* section can be used for discussion.

   • Students discuss the questions in small groups and then write their individual responses on the blackline masters or using the *Evaluation and Tracking Software.*

• The teacher may score the response using a variety of rubrics. For example, the teacher could give points for all reasonable responses in complete sentences that begin with a capital letter and end with appropriate punctuation.

2. For certain students, the teacher may ask the questions and prompt the student to give a thoughtful oral response.

3. Another option is to use *Think About It* as a mini-assessment. Have the students answer the questions independently on paper or using the *Evaluation and Tracking Software.*

The *Write About It* section gives students extended practice writing about what they have read. Students may write for as long as time allows.

The students may answer on the blackline master or use the *Evaluation and Tracking Software.* To motivate students, the *Evaluation and Tracking Software* includes a spelling checker and a variety of fonts and colors for students to choose from. This section is teacher-scored. Scores may be entered on a copy of the **Individual Progress Chart** or on the *Evaluation and Tracking Software.*

Students may keep their essays in a writing portfolio. At the end of the term students choose one of their essays to improve using the writing process. The final question in each *Write About It* section asks students to complete one of the graphic organizers that can be found as blackline masters in the back of this *Teacher's Guide* or on the *Evaluation and Tracking Software.* Graphic organizers are a structured, alternative writing experience. There are Book Report Forms, a What I Know/What I Learned Chart, a Sequencing Chart, and so on. Scores may be entered on the blackline master or *Evaluation and Tracking Software* version of the **Individual Progress Chart.**

Individual Progress Chart

Enter the percentage correct score for each quiz or activity.

Name: _____ Class: _____

Book Title	Building Background	Chapter 1 Quiz	Chapter 2 Quiz	Chapter 3 Quiz	Chapter 4 Quiz	Chapter 5 Quiz	Chapter 6 Quiz	Thinking and Writing	Graphic Organizer
Adventures on the Nile									
Hyperlinking through the Solar System									
Seven Wonders of the World									
Race to Space									
Around the World									
Earth Belongs to You									
Treasure Island									
Gulliver's Travels									

Anything's Possible

3

Name: _____ Class: _____

Fluency Graph

WCPM RATE
Number of words read correctly in one minute

10 20 30 40 50 60 70 80 90 100 110 120 130 140 150 160 170 180

Date

ERRORS

Above 6 | 6 | 5 | 4 | 3 | 2 | 1 | 0

1. Read a fluency passage for one minute. 2. Find the next open column. 3. Color the column to the number that shows how far you read.
4. Mark the number of errors in the chart at the bottom.

Book Summaries

Adventures on the Nile

By Andrew Cameron

Summary

When Maria writes a winning essay about animals, she joins five other students for a trip along the Nile River. The students and their chaperone meet with their tour guide, Miss Salam, in Ethiopia. Then they travel through Sudan into Egypt. On each leg of the journey they encounter animals that live in and around the Nile River. In addition to learning the traits and habitats of these animals, readers learn about the cultures, ancient societies, and legends of the people who inhabit the shores of the Nile River.

Literary Terms

Adventure: realistic characters and events; emphasizes action and suspense; setting is a real place or a place that could be real; sometimes includes a chase or attempt to find some object or reach a specific goal

Setting: the story environment; its time and place

Other Resources

Book: Hoy, Susan. *Journey Up the Nile* (Traveling Bear Press, 1999)

Movie: *Mystery of the Nile* (2004)

Web site: http://www.nileriver.com/nile/nileinfo/nileinfo.htm

Hyperlinking through the Solar System

By Jennifer Weinstein

Summary

Mr. Todd, a very creative science teacher, uses hyperlinks on his Web site to give his class a close-up lesson on the solar system. Directing this lesson is a NASA astronomer who takes the students on a rocket trip from Mars to Saturn to the dwarf planet Pluto. The students see the mountains and valleys of Mars, hear asteroids beating against their rocket, see the rings of Saturn, experience the low gravity of Pluto, and see a comet before returning to the computer lab where their lesson began.

Literary Term

Science Fiction: an adventure story often set in other times or on other planets; often includes advanced technology, spaceships, robots, or aliens

Other Resources

Book: Davis, Kenneth C. and Pedro Martin. *Don't Know Much about the Solar System* (HarperCollins, 2001)

Movie: *Wheels on Mars* (2004)

Web site: http://www.kidsastronomy.com/solar_system.htm

Seven Wonders of the World

By Nick Pease

Summary

Only one of the original Seven Wonders of the World still exists. There are, however, some existing examples of beauty and creativity. The Great Wall of China, the city of Petra in present-day Jordan, Angkor Wat in Cambodia, and India's Taj Mahal are offered as other wonders still able to be seen. Wonders in the Western Hemisphere include the lines and pictures of Nazca, which can be seen in their entirety only from the air, the statues of Easter Island, and the modern city of Brasilia.

Literary Term

Nonfiction: a factual piece of literature

Other Resources

Book: Cazet, Denys. *Minnie & Moo and the Seven Wonders of the World* (Atheneum/Richard Jackson Books, 2003)

Movie: *A&E Seven Wonders of the World* (1997)

Web site: http://library.thinkquest.org/J002388/index.html

Race to Space

By C. L. Collins

Summary

Following World War II, the United States and the Soviet Union competed against each other in the exploration of space. In 1957 the Soviet Union launched the first satellite, *Sputnik*. The United States launched its first satellite, *Explorer*, in 1958. The Soviet Union put the first man in space on April 12, 1961; the United States' first manned space flight occurred on May 5, 1961. The United States landed the first man on the moon in 1969. Today many countries participate in space exploration on the International Space Station.

Literary Terms

Nonfiction: a factual piece of literature

Foreshadowing: an author's hints about events that will occur later in the story

Other Resources

Book: Leonov, Alexei and David Scott. *Two Sides of the Moon: Our Story of the Cold War Space Race* (Thomas Dunne Books, 2004)

Movie: *Race to Space* (2001)

Web Site: http://www.cdli.ca/CITE/spaceexplorers.htm

Anything's Possible

Around the World

By Elizabeth Laskey

Summary

From the time of Ferdinand Magellan to the present, the desire, determination, and bravery it takes to sail around the globe has inspired many. Not long after airplanes came into use, pilots began to fly around the world, eventually without even having to refuel. Improvements to hot-air balloons also inspired some people to float around the globe. Still other travelers use only "human power" to propel them on their quest to circle the globe. For example, one man walked around the world. Others have added skates, bicycles, and pedal-powered boats to the journey.

Literary Terms

Nonfiction: a factual piece of literature

Biography: an account of a person's life written by another person

Other Resources

Book: Goodman, Joan Elizabeth and Tom McNeely. *A Long and Uncertain Journey: The 27,000-Mile Voyage of Vasco Da Gama* (Mikaya Press, 2001)

Movie: *Around the World in 80 Days* (2004)

Web Site: http://www.didyouknow.cd/aroundtheworld/sailing.htm

Earth Belongs to You

By Jane Davin

Summary

Readers are introduced to the idea that they have a responsibility to take care of Earth. Global warming, caused by too much carbon dioxide in the air, is causing some of Earth's ice and snow to melt. Global warming has brought severe weather problems. There are ways to help reduce global warming, such as recycling. Readers are given a look into a brighter future where cars run on electricity and levels of carbon dioxide in the air have been reduced.

Literary Term

Nonfiction: a factual piece of literature

Other Resources

Book: Swartz, Linda. *Earth for Kids: Activities to Help Heal the Environment* (Learning Works, 1990)

Movie: *Earth Aid: Recycling* (2006)

Web Site: http://epa.gov/climatechange/kids/index.html

Treasure Island

Retold by Nick Pease

Summary

Young Jim Hawkins faces risk and adventure in this story that begins when a sea captain leaves Jim a treasure chest containing a highly sought-after treasure map. Jim and his friends must figure out a way to get to the treasure before pirates get to them. Through an incidental meeting with a man named Ben Gunn and Jim's schemes to outwit the pirates, Jim and his friends are able to stay alive and bring the treasure home while leaving the pirates stranded on a deserted island.

Author

Robert Louis Stevenson (1850–1894) wrote *Treasure Island* in 1881. Born in Scotland, Stevenson eventually traveled to the South Seas where he spent the last years of his life. *Treasure Island* originally began as a game with his stepson, but soon grew into a tale of adventure and a commentary on the ambiguity of human motives.

Literary Term

Suspense: arousing the reader's curiosity or making the reader wonder what will happen next

Other Resources

Book: Girard, Geoffrey. *Tales of the Atlantic Pirates* (Middle Atlantic Press, 2006)

Web Site: http://www.online-literature.com/stevenson/treasureisland/

Gulliver's Travels

Retold by Robert Logan

Summary

Gulliver, an English doctor, has many adventures after his ship crashes during a storm. He first finds himself the captive of the Lilliputians, a race of tiny people. While there, he helps avert war between two nations. Another time Gulliver finds himself in Brobdingnag, a land of giants. He is sold to the queen of Brobdingnag, where life is pleasant but unsafe. Gulliver returns to sea and eventually makes his way back to England.

Author

Gulliver's Travels was originally written by Jonathan Swift (1667–1745), an Irish author. Swift is famous for his satires. *Gulliver's Travels* contains humorous stories about royalty, politics, and human behavior. Although intended for adults, its creative plot has also made it a favorite story for young people.

Literary Terms

Setting: the story environment; its time and place

Flashback: a past event that is told out of order

Other Resources

Movie: *Gulliver's Travels* (1939)

Web site: http://www.online-literature.com/swift/gulliver/

Name _____ Date _____

Adventures on the Nile
What You Know

Write answers to these questions.

1. What animals live near rivers? _____

   _____

2. What do you think it would be like to live next to a big river? _____

   _____

3. Which African animal do you think is the most dangerous? Why?

   _____

4. What countries are located on the Nile River? _____

   _____

5. If you could travel to Egypt, what would you like to see? _____

   _____

Word Meanings
Definitions

Look for these words as you read your chapter book. When you find one of these words, write its definition.

crocodile: _____

flute: _____

fossil: _____

giraffe: _____

spooky: _____

Adventures on the Nile

Unfamiliar Words	Word Meanings	Proper Nouns	
chirping, countries, eggshell, hatch, won, wrote	crocodile	Brazil, Egypt, Ethiopia, Miss Salam, Nile River	Chapter 1
hippo, important, rhino, tusks, voice		Africa, Kamiko, Japan	Chapter 2
counted, danger, farther, group, languages, tongue	giraffe	Dinder National Park, Nadir, Sudan	Chapter 3
change, claws, desert, pointed, poisonous, pyramid, raised, scorpion	fossil	Egyptian, Africa, Finland	Chapter 4
ancient, cobra, flute, *neilos*	flute	Greek, Harini, India	Chapter 5
adventure, squeaked, torches, treasures	spooky	Great Sphinx	Chapter 6

Name _____ Date _____

Adventures on the Nile
Chapter 1, "Ricardo's Crocodile"

Mark each statement *T* for true or *F* for false.

_____ **1.** The children start their journey in Somalia, where the Nile River originates.

_____ **2.** The Nile River is about 4000 miles long.

_____ **3.** The Nile River is as long as the United States is wide.

_____ **4.** Crocodiles can be up to 20 feet long.

_____ **5.** Crocodiles can weigh up to 20,000 pounds.

_____ **6.** Crocodiles have been around for over 300 million years.

_____ **7.** Female crocodiles lay 25 to 80 eggs in the water.

_____ **8.** A mother crocodile stays with her baby crocodiles for a long time.

_____ **9.** A mother crocodile protects her babies by putting them in her mouth.

_____ **10.** Baby crocodiles do not make any sounds as they hatch.

Read the question, and write your answer.

What does this chapter tell us about the Nile River?

_____

_____

Name _____ Date _____

Adventures on the Nile
Chapter 2, "Kamiko's Hippo"

Fill in the bubble beside the answer for each question.

1. The country of Ethiopia is
   - Ⓐ surrounded by land.
   - Ⓑ surrounded by rivers.
   - Ⓒ flat and dry.

2. The only two land animals that are bigger than the hippo are
   - Ⓐ rhinos and elephants.
   - Ⓑ elephants and giraffes.
   - Ⓒ rhinos and giraffes.

3. The two parts of the Nile River are
   - Ⓐ the Blue Nile and the Green Nile.
   - Ⓑ the White Nile and the Blue Nile.
   - Ⓒ the Green Nile and the Red Nile.

4. Baby hippos are
   - Ⓐ born in water.
   - Ⓑ over 100 pounds at birth.
   - Ⓒ able to stay under water for ten minutes at birth.

Read the question, and write your answer.

Describe three traits of hippos. _____

_____

_____

Name _____ Date _____

Adventures on the Nile
Chapter 3, "Nadir's Giraffe"

Number the events in order from 1 to 5.

_____ The students visited Dinder National Park near the Ethiopian border.

_____ The students learned that there are more than 600 people groups and 400 languages in Sudan.

_____ Nadir, a boy from Turkey, taught the students about the giraffe.

_____ The group left Ethiopia and traveled to Sudan.

_____ They met the tallest animal in Africa, the giraffe.

Mark each statement *T* for true or *F* for false.

_____ 1. A giraffe's tongue can be up to 21 inches long.

_____ 2. A giraffe can be as tall as 30 feet.

_____ 3. The spots on a giraffe's skin help it hide in the trees.

_____ 4. Giraffes sometimes stay in herds, which can be as small as ten or as large as 70.

Read the question, and write your answer.

What physical traits of a giraffe help protect it from danger?

_____

_____

Name _____ Date _____

Adventures on the Nile
Chapter 4, "Peter's Scorpion"

Mark each statement *T* for true or *F* for false.

_____ 1. Sudan is the biggest country in Africa.

_____ 2. The only country in Africa with pyramids is Egypt.

_____ 3. Scorpions live in hot, dry, desert environments.

_____ 4. The scorpion has a pointed tail with three stingers.

_____ 5. Scorpions can be brown, yellow, or white.

_____ 6. Brown scorpions are the most poisonous.

_____ 7. Scorpions are good, efficient hunters.

_____ 8. Scorpions almost never need food.

_____ 9. Scorpions have changed greatly over time.

_____ 10. Scorpions are called "living fossils" because they look like real fossils.

Read the question, and write your answer.

What do some Egyptians believe about scorpions?

_____

_____

Name _____ Date _____

Adventures on the Nile
Chapter 5, "Harini's Cobra"

Number the events in order from 1 to 5.

_____ The group walked to a market where they saw many things for sale.

_____ They saw odd shows including a snake charmer.

_____ Mr. Davis explained that the name "Nile" comes from the Greek word *neilos,* which means "river valley."

_____ The group left Sudan and went into Egypt.

_____ Harini, a student from India, explained that she had seen snake charmers before.

Number the events in order from 6 to 10.

_____ Harini explained that cobras stand up to look bigger.

_____ The students were afraid when they saw the head of the cobra rise out of the basket.

_____ The snake charmer began to play a flute.

_____ Harini told the students that many snake charmers remove the snake's fangs.

_____ A man removed the lid from a basket.

Read the question, and write your answer.

What are two of the traits that distinguish cobras?

_____

_____

Name _____ Date _____

Adventures on the Nile
Chapter 6, "Maria's Cat"

Fill in the bubble beside the answer for each question.

1. The Great Sphinx is a
   - Ⓐ big marble cat.
   - Ⓑ big stone cat body with the head of a king.
   - Ⓒ one of Egypt's most famous pyramids.

2. Cats were important to ancient Egyptians because they
   - Ⓐ were good hunters and could see well at night.
   - Ⓑ made good pets.
   - Ⓒ were good at keeping things safe.

3. Some people believe that the Great Sphinx is part cat because ancient Egyptians believed
   - Ⓐ cats kept snakes and rats away.
   - Ⓑ cats could heal them.
   - Ⓒ the cat was a magical creature.

4. Why is the Great Sphinx missing its nose?
   - Ⓐ It was smashed by an upset king.
   - Ⓑ The wind and the rain slowly eroded it away.
   - Ⓒ No one really knows.

Read the question, and write your answer.

Name some of the treasures of Egypt. _____

_____

_____

Name _____ Date _____

Adventures on the Nile
Think About It

Write about or give an oral presentation for each question.

1. How do the animals that live along the Nile River differ from those that live in the desert?

   _____

2. How were the interiors of the pyramids decorated? Why do you think they were decorated this way?

   _____

3. Why is it important to learn about different animals and their habitats?

   _____

4. Compare and contrast the scorpion and the crocodile. Be sure to include what they have in common as well as their differences.

   _____

   _____

Write About It

Choose one of the questions below. Write your answer on a sheet of paper.

1. Draw a map of Africa. Show the Nile River and the countries the students visited. Write a paragraph explaining the direction in which the students traveled and how long you think it took the group to travel from place to place.

2. Compare and contrast the different countries the students visited.

3. Complete the Book Report Form for this book.

Adventures on the Nile

Chapter 1 *page 3*

*Not long after we left the shore we spotted some crocodiles. A	12
student from Brazil named Ricardo told us that crocodiles can be up to	25
20 feet long and 2,000 pounds.	31

"That's right," Miss Salam said. "And they have been around for	42
more than 200 million years." Miss Salam led the boat closer to shore.	55

"Look! There are eggs!" Ricardo shouted. He said that the mother	66
crocodile lays 25 to 80 eggs in a nest. After they hatch, she stays with the	82
babies for a long time. She puts the* babies in her mouth when she needs	97
to keep them safe.	101

Chapter 4 *page 16*

*"It can be hard to see, but the scorpion really has two stingers at the	15
end of its tail," Peter told us. "It also has two big claws. Scorpions can be	31
brown, yellow, or white. The white ones are the most poisonous." This	43
scorpion was brown.	46

Unlike the other animals we had seen, the scorpion was not big. Its	59
body was only about three inches long. Mr. Davis told us that some	72
Egyptians believe scorpions help heal sick people.	79

"Scorpions are not very good hunters," Miss Salam said. "They	89
almost* never need food, so they can wait a very long time between	102
meals."	103

- The target rate for **Anything's Possible** is 90 wcpm. The asterisks (*) mark 90 words.

- Listen to the student read the passage. Count the number of words read in one minute and the number of errors.

- For the reading rate, subtract the number of errors from the total number of words read.

- Have students enter their scores on their **Fluency Graph.** See page 9.

Answer Key

Building Background

Name _____ Date _____

Adventures on the Nile
What You Know

Write answers to these questions.

1. What animals live near rivers? _____
   Accept reasonable responses.

2. What do you think it would be like to live next to a big river? ____
   Accept reasonable responses.

3. Which African animal do you think is the most dangerous? Why?
   Accept reasonable responses.

4. What countries are located on the Nile River? _____
   Ideas: Ethiopia, Sudan, Egypt

5. If you could travel to Egypt, what would you like to see? _____
   Accept reasonable responses.

Word Meanings
Definitions

Look for these words as you read your chapter book. When you find one of these words, write its definition.

crocodile: **a large reptile with a long body and tail, tough skin, a long, pointed snout, and four short legs**

flute: **a woodwind instrument with a high pitch**

fossil: **the remains, prints, or traces of plants and animals that lived long ago**

giraffe: **a large African animal that has a very long neck, long legs, and a spotted coat**

spooky: **weird; eerie**

12   Anything's Possible • Book 1

Adventures on the Nile

Chapter Quiz

Name _____ Date _____

Adventures on the Nile
Chapter 1, "Ricardo's Crocodile"

Mark each statement *T* for true or *F* for false.

_F_ 1. The children start their journey in Somalia, where the Nile River originates.

_T_ 2. The Nile River is about 4000 miles long.

_T_ 3. The Nile River is as long as the United States is wide.

_T_ 4. Crocodiles can be up to 20 feet long.

_F_ 5. Crocodiles can weigh up to 20,000 pounds.

_F_ 6. Crocodiles have been around for over 300 million years.

_F_ 7. Female crocodiles lay 25 to 80 eggs in the water.

_T_ 8. A mother crocodile stays with her baby crocodiles for a long time.

_T_ 9. A mother crocodile protects her babies by putting them in her mouth.

_F_ 10. Baby crocodiles do not make any sounds as they hatch.

Read the question, and write your answer.

What does this chapter tell us about the Nile River?
Ideas: It is a very long, navigable river in Africa; it is home to many animals, including crocodiles.

14   Anything's Possible • Book 1

Adventures on the Nile

Chapter Quiz

Name _____ Date _____

Adventures on the Nile
Chapter 2, "Kamiko's Hippo"

Fill in the bubble beside the answer for each question.

1. The country of Ethiopia is
   - ● surrounded by land.
   - Ⓑ surrounded by rivers.
   - Ⓒ flat and dry.

2. The only two land animals that are bigger than the hippo are
   - ● rhinos and elephants.
   - Ⓑ elephants and giraffes.
   - Ⓒ rhinos and giraffes.

3. The two parts of the Nile River are
   - Ⓐ the Blue Nile and the Green Nile.
   - ● the White Nile and the Blue Nile.
   - Ⓒ the Green Nile and the Red Nile.

4. Baby hippos are
   - ● born in water.
   - Ⓑ over 100 pounds at birth.
   - Ⓒ able to stay under water for ten minutes at birth.

Read the question, and write your answer.

Describe three traits of hippos. **They can have foot-long tusks and are one of the three largest land animals in Africa. Baby hippos are born under water and can stay there for up to five minutes.**

Anything's Possible • Book 1   15

Adventures on the Nile

Chapter Quiz

Name _____ Date _____

Adventures on the Nile
Chapter 3, "Nadir's Giraffe"

Number the events in order from 1 to 5.

_3_ The students visited Dinder National Park near the Ethiopian border.

_2_ The students learned that there are more than 600 people groups and 400 languages in Sudan.

_5_ Nadir, a boy from Turkey, taught the students about the giraffe.

_1_ The group left Ethiopia and traveled to Sudan.

_4_ They met the tallest animal in Africa, the giraffe.

Mark each statement *T* for true or *F* for false.

_T_ 1. A giraffe's tongue can be up to 21 inches long.

_F_ 2. A giraffe can be as tall as 30 feet.

_T_ 3. The spots on a giraffe's skin help it hide in the trees.

_T_ 4. Giraffes sometimes stay in herds, which can be as small as ten or as large as 70.

Read the question, and write your answer.

What physical traits of a giraffe help protect it from danger?
Ideas: good eyesight; tall so it can see long distances; long legs help it run fast; spots help it hide

16   Anything's Possible • Book 1

Adventures on the Nile

Chapter Quiz

Name _____ Date _____

Adventures on the Nile
Chapter 4, "Peter's Scorpion"

Mark each statement *T* for true or *F* for false.

T 1. Sudan is the biggest country in Africa.

F 2. The only country in Africa with pyramids is Egypt.

T 3. Scorpions live in hot, dry, desert environments.

F 4. The scorpion has a pointed tail with three stingers.

T 5. Scorpions can be brown, yellow, or white.

F 6. Brown scorpions are the most poisonous.

F 7. Scorpions are good, efficient hunters.

T 8. Scorpions almost never need food.

F 9. Scorpions have changed greatly over time.

T 10. Scorpions are called "living fossils" because they look like real fossils.

Read the question, and write your answer.

What do some Egyptians believe about scorpions?
They believe scorpions can heal sick people.

Anything's Possible • Book 1   17

Adventures on the Nile

Chapter Quiz

Name _____ Date _____

Adventures on the Nile
Chapter 5, "Harini's Cobra"

Number the events in order from 1 to 5.

3 The group walked to a market where they saw many things for sale.

4 They saw odd shows including a snake charmer.

2 Mr. Davis explained that the name "Nile" comes from the Greek word *neilos,* which means "river valley."

1 The group left Sudan and went into Egypt.

5 Harini, a student from India, explained that she had seen snake charmers before.

Number the events in order from 6 to 10.

10 Harini explained that cobras stand up to look bigger.

8 The students were afraid when they saw the head of the cobra rise out of the basket.

6 The snake charmer began to play a flute.

9 Harini told the students that many snake charmers remove the snake's fangs.

7 A man removed the lid from a basket.

Read the question, and write your answer.

What are two of the traits that distinguish cobras?
Ideas: can grow up to eight feet long; cobra stands and opens
its hood when it is scared

18   Anything's Possible • Book 1

Adventures on the Nile

Chapter Quiz

Name _____ Date _____

Adventures on the Nile
Chapter 6, "Maria's Cat"

Fill in the bubble beside the answer for each question.

1. The Great Sphinx is a
   Ⓐ big marble cat.
   ● big stone cat body with the head of a king.
   Ⓒ one of Egypt's most famous pyramids.

2. Cats were important to ancient Egyptians because they
   Ⓐ were good hunters and could see well at night.
   Ⓑ made good pets.
   ● were good at keeping things safe.

3. Some people believe that the Great Sphinx is part cat because ancient Egyptians believed
   ● cats kept snakes and rats away.
   Ⓑ cats could heal them.
   Ⓒ the cat was a magical creature.

4. Why is the Great Sphinx missing its nose?
   Ⓐ It was smashed by an upset king.
   Ⓑ The wind and the rain slowly eroded it away.
   ● No one really knows.

Read the question, and write your answer.

Name some of the treasures of Egypt. **Ideas: the Great Sphinx; the**
pyramids; paintings inside the pyramids

Anything's Possible • Book 1   19

Adventures on the Nile

Thinking and Writing

Name _____ Date _____

Adventures on the Nile
Think About It

Write about or give an oral presentation for each question.

1. How do the animals that live along the Nile River differ from those that live in the desert?
   Accept reasonable responses.

2. How were the interiors of the pyramids decorated? Why do you think they were decorated this way?
   Idea: with paintings; accept other reasonable responses

3. Why is it important to learn about different animals and their habitats?
   Accept reasonable responses.

4. Compare and contrast the scorpion and the crocodile. Be sure to include what they have in common as well as their differences.
   Ideas: similar: neither has changed much over time, both have
   been around for millions of years; differences: size, habitat

Write About It

Choose one of the questions below. Write your answer on a sheet of paper.

1. Draw a map of Africa. Show the Nile River and the countries the students visited. Write a paragraph explaining the direction in which the students traveled and how long you think it took the group to travel from place to place.

2. Compare and contrast the different countries the students visited. **Answers should be based on information in the book.**

3. Complete the Book Report Form for this book.

20   Anything's Possible • Book 1

Adventures on the Nile

Name _____ Date _____

Hyperlinking through the Solar System
What You Know

Write answers to these questions.

1. What is a solar system? Name three planets in our solar system.

   _____

   _____

   _____

2. Pluto is now considered a dwarf planet. Conduct research on Pluto
   and list some of the differences between it and normal planets.

   _____

   _____

3. List at least two ways people study space. _____

   _____

   _____

Word Meanings
Synonyms

**Look for these words as you read your chapter book. When you find a
word, write a synonym for the word.**

excellent: _____

canyon: _____

alien: _____

object: _____

catch: _____

journey: _____

Hyperlinking through the Solar System

	Unfamiliar Words	Word Meanings	Proper Nouns
Chapter 1	asteroid computer friends galaxy hyperlink learn science solar system	excellent	Diana Javier Jazmyn Jupiter Mars Mercury Milky Way Neptune Saturn Simon Uranus Venus
Chapter 2	astronomer martians mountains robots rovers suit	alien canyon	Deimos Maria Sanchez NASA Phobos
Chapter 3	comets		Ceres
Chapter 4	dwarf planet known since	object	
Chapter 5	gravity space voice	catch	Pluto
Chapter 6		journey	

Name _____ Date _____

Hyperlinking through the Solar System
Chapter 1, "The Science Lesson"

Mark each statement *T* for true or *F* for false.

_____ **1.** Mr. Todd teaches science.

_____ **2.** Mr. Todd's class always meets in the computer lab.

_____ **3.** The class is beginning a new lesson on insects.

_____ **4.** It is always easy to tell in advance what Mr. Todd's classes are about.

_____ **5.** The Milky Way is the name of a planet.

_____ **6.** Earth and many other planets make up our solar system.

_____ **7.** There are stars, planets, and asteroids in the Milky Way.

_____ **8.** The phrase "My very excellent mother just stacked up nachos" helps students remember the names of the moons of Jupiter.

_____ **9.** There are eight planets in our solar system.

_____ **10.** The students disappeared when they clicked on the words *solar system*.

Read the question, and write your answer.

How are a solar system and a galaxy related?

_____

_____

Name _____ Date _____

Hyperlinking through the Solar System
Chapter 2, "Seeing Red"

Fill in the bubble beside the answer for each question.

1. Astronomers are scientists who
   Ⓐ study stars, planets, and other things in space.
   Ⓑ study rocks, mountains, and craters.
   Ⓒ build spaceships.

2. The mountains and canyons on Mars
   Ⓐ make the ones on Earth look big.
   Ⓑ make the ones on Earth look small.
   Ⓒ look just like the ones on Earth.

3. The two moons of Mars are
   Ⓐ Luna and Phobos.
   Ⓑ Deimos and Saturn.
   Ⓒ Phobos and Deimos.

4. Rovers are
   Ⓐ robots sent to Mars by NASA.
   Ⓑ scientists who work at many jobs.
   Ⓒ robots sent by NASA to explore the Milky Way.

Read the question, and write your answer.

Name three things the students learned about Mars. _____

_____

_____

_____

Name _____ Date _____

Hyperlinking through the Solar System
Chapter 3, "Things Get Rocky"

Number the events in order from 1 to 5.

_____ The students sat quietly and waited to reach Saturn.

_____ The students heard a loud *bang* as something hit the rocket.

_____ The banging stopped as the rocket left the asteroid belt.

_____ The rocket left Mars for the outer solar system.

_____ The students saw rocks floating around the rocket.

Mark each statement *T* for true or *F* for false.

_____ 1. The asteroid belt is between Jupiter and Saturn.

_____ 2. Asteroids are rocks that orbit the sun.

_____ 3. Asteroids can be over 500 kilometers wide.

_____ 4. Most of the asteroids in the solar system are between Earth and Mars.

Read the question, and write your answer.

How do the author's words help you feel the asteroids hitting the ship?

_____

_____

_____

Name _____ Date _____

Hyperlinking through the Solar System
Chapter 4, "To Saturn"

Fill in the bubble beside the answer for each question.

1. Javier was surprised that
   - Ⓐ Saturn looked so small.
   - Ⓑ Saturn's rings are made of many objects.
   - Ⓒ Saturn's rings are made of only giant rocks.

2. Which of these planets has rings?
   - Ⓐ Jupiter
   - Ⓑ Uranus
   - Ⓒ both A and B

3. What is the largest planet in our solar system?
   - Ⓐ Mars
   - Ⓑ Saturn
   - Ⓒ Jupiter

4. How many moons does Saturn have?
   - Ⓐ none
   - Ⓑ two
   - Ⓒ around 30

Read the question, and write your answer.

Describe what Saturn's rings are made of. _____

_____

_____

_____

Name _____ Date _____

Hyperlinking through the Solar System
Chapter 5, "A Dwarf Planet"

Mark each statement *T* for true or *F* for false.

_____ **1.** The Milky Way contains nine planets.

_____ **2.** When scientists learned more about Pluto, they decided it was not the same as the other planets.

_____ **3.** Pluto may have been one of Neptune's moons.

_____ **4.** Pluto is now called a dwarf planet.

_____ **5.** Pluto is the closest planet to Earth.

_____ **6.** It takes nine years to go from Earth to Pluto.

_____ **7.** The students were much heavier on Pluto than on Earth.

_____ **8.** The class needed space suits and helmets to go onto Pluto.

_____ **9.** The students were eager to go home.

_____ **10.** Simon clicked on the last link—*Home*.

Read the question, and write your answer.

Why were the students able to pick each other up so easily on Pluto?

_____

_____

_____

Name _____ Date _____

Hyperlinking through the Solar System
Chapter 6, "The Journey Ends"

Number the events in order from 1 to 5.

_____ A comet passed the rocket.

_____ The students were back in the computer lab.

_____ The rocket left Pluto.

_____ Dr. Sanchez pressed a button on the computer and there was
a sudden flash of light.

_____ The students took off their space suits and sat down.

Mark each statement *T* for true or *F* for false.

_____ 1. A comet contains frozen ice, gases, and dust.

_____ 2. A comet orbits the planet it is closest to.

_____ 3. Mr. Todd does odd things sometimes.

_____ 4. The students needed to wear space suits in the rocket ship.

Read the question, and write your answer.

Why do you think the author used fiction and nonfiction together in this story?

_____

_____

_____

Name _____ Date _____

Hyperlinking through the Solar System
Think About It

Write about or give an oral presentation for each question.

1. How can you explore the galaxy using hyperlinks?

   _____

   _____

   _____

2. How would gravity on Jupiter compare to gravity on Pluto?

   _____

   _____

3. How are the asteroid belt, the rings of Saturn, and a comet similar?

   _____

   _____

Write About It

Choose one of the questions below. Write your answer on a sheet of paper.

1. If you could explore our solar system, where would you go? Write a letter to a friend telling where you would want to explore and what you would want to learn.

2. Imagine you are an astronomer from 1650 and you have just been transported to the present time. You spent the day at a planetarium studying the rings of Saturn with a NASA astronomer. Write a one-page diary entry telling about what you learned and why you didn't know that in 1650.

3. Complete the Genres Chart for this book.

Anything's Possible • Book 2

Hyperlinking through the Solar System

Chapter 3 *pages 14 and 15*

*The class looked out the window. They saw rocks floating around	11
the rocket.	13
"We must be in the asteroid belt between Mars and Jupiter," Dr.	25
Sanchez told them. "Most of the asteroids in the solar system are here."	38
"Look! There is a really big one over there!" Simon yelled.	49
"Yes, that is a big one," Dr. Sanchez said. "But it is not the biggest	64
asteroid. The biggest asteroid is named Ceres. It is 933 kilometers wide."	76
The banging stopped. The rocket was leaving the asteroid belt.	86
Diana helped Jazmyn pick* herself up off the floor. The other students	98
were also getting up.	102

Chapter 5 *pages 24 and 25*

*Students started picking up their friends. Two boys began playing	10
catch with Simon. Simon was laughing inside his helmet.	19
"Boys, please set him down," Dr. Sanchez said.	27
"Look over there!" Diana shouted. "Is that another dwarf planet?"	37
"No, that is Neptune," Dr. Sanchez answered. "Astronomers think	46
Pluto may have been one of Neptune's moons a long time ago."	58
"You said nobody has ever been to Pluto before. Why not?" Jazmyn	70
asked.	71
"It takes nine years to go from Earth to Pluto," Dr. Sanchez said.	84
"We have been gone for nine* years?" Jazmyn asked with wide eyes.	96
Dr. Sanchez smiled and looked at her watch.	104

- The target rate for **Anything's Possible** is 90 wcpm. The asterisks (*) mark 90 words.
- Listen to the student read the passage. Count the number of words read in one minute and the number of errors.
- For the reading rate, subtract the number of errors from the total number of words read.
- Have students enter their scores on their **Fluency Graph.** See page 9.

Answer Key

Name _____ Date _____

Hyperlinking through the Solar System
What You Know

Write answers to these questions.

1. What is a solar system? Name three planets in our solar system.
   a group of planets, moons, comets, and asteroids that move
   around a sun; accept any three of the following: Mercury,
   Venus, Earth, Mars, Jupiter, Saturn, Uranus, or Neptune

2. Pluto is now considered a dwarf planet. Conduct research on Pluto and list some of the differences between it and normal planets.
   Students' answers should show an understanding of the
   differences between a dwarf planet and a normal planet.

3. List at least two ways people study space.
   Ideas: naked eye, telescope, unmanned craft, space station,
   spacecraft, the Hubble telescope

Word Meanings
Synonyms

Look for these words as you read your chapter book. When you find a word, write a synonym for the word.

excellent: **Ideas: super, great**

canyon: **Ideas: gorge, ravine**

alien: **Ideas: extraterrestrial, otherworldly**

object: **Ideas: thing, item**

catch: **Idea: grab, take hold of**

journey: **Ideas: trip, expedition**

24   Anything's Possible • Book 2

Name _____ Date _____

Hyperlinking through the Solar System
Chapter 1, "The Science Lesson"

Mark each statement *T* for true or *F* for false.

T 1. Mr. Todd teaches science.

F 2. Mr. Todd's class always meets in the computer lab.

F 3. The class is beginning a new lesson on insects.

F 4. It is always easy to tell in advance what Mr. Todd's classes are about.

F 5. The Milky Way is the name of a planet.

T 6. Earth and many other planets make up our solar system.

T 7. There are stars, planets, and asteroids in the Milky Way.

F 8. The phrase "My very excellent mother just stacked up nachos" helps students remember the names of the moons of Jupiter.

T 9. There are eight planets in our solar system.

T 10. The students disappeared when they clicked on the words *solar system*.

Read the question, and write your answer.

How are a solar system and a galaxy related?
A solar system is one part of a galaxy.

26   Anything's Possible • Book 2

Name _____ Date _____

Hyperlinking through the Solar System
Chapter 2, "Seeing Red"

Fill in the bubble beside the answer for each question.

1. Astronomers are scientists who
   ● study stars, planets, and other things in space.
   Ⓑ study rocks, mountains, and craters.
   Ⓒ build spaceships.

2. The mountains and canyons on Mars
   Ⓐ make the ones on Earth look big.
   ● make the ones on Earth look small.
   Ⓒ look just like the ones on Earth.

3. The two moons of Mars are
   Ⓐ Luna and Phobos.
   Ⓑ Deimos and Saturn.
   ● Phobos and Deimos.

4. Rovers are
   ● robots sent to Mars by NASA.
   Ⓑ scientists who work at many jobs.
   Ⓒ robots sent by NASA to explore the Milky Way.

Read the question, and write your answer.

Name three things the students learned about Mars. **Accept any**
three of the following: it is big and red; its mountains and
canyons are big; it has two moons; NASA has sent rovers to
that planet.

Anything's Possible • Book 2   27

Name _____ Date _____

Hyperlinking through the Solar System
Chapter 3, "Things Get Rocky"

Number the events in order from 1 to 5.

5 The students sat quietly and waited to reach Saturn.

2 The students heard a loud *bang* as something hit the rocket.

4 The banging stopped as the rocket left the asteroid belt.

1 The rocket left Mars for the outer solar system.

3 The students saw rocks floating around the rocket.

Mark each statement *T* for true or *F* for false.

F 1. The asteroid belt is between Jupiter and Saturn.

T 2. Asteroids are rocks that orbit the sun.

T 3. Asteroids can be over 500 kilometers wide.

F 4. Most of the asteroids in the solar system are between Earth and Mars.

Read the question, and write your answer.

How do the author's words help you feel the asteroids hitting the ship?
Reasonable responses may include: the author's use of italics
to say *bang*; descriptions of the ship rocking from side to side;
students falling to the floor

28   Anything's Possible • Book 2

Chapter Quiz

Name _____ **Date** _____

Hyperlinking through the Solar System
Chapter 4, "To Saturn"

Fill in the bubble beside the answer for each question.

1. Javier was surprised that
   Ⓐ Saturn looked so small.
   ● Saturn's rings are made of many objects.
   Ⓒ Saturn's rings are made of only giant rocks.

2. Which of these planets has rings?
   Ⓐ Jupiter
   Ⓑ Uranus
   ● both A and B

3. What is the largest planet in our solar system?
   Ⓐ Mars
   Ⓑ Saturn
   ● Jupiter

4. How many moons does Saturn have?
   Ⓐ none
   Ⓑ two
   ● around 30

Read the question, and write your answer.

Describe what Saturn's rings are made of. __They are made of__
millions of objects, from very tiny to very big. The objects are
probably ice.

Anything's Possible • Book 2   29

Hyperlinking through the Solar System

Chapter Quiz

Name _____ **Date** _____

Hyperlinking through the Solar System
Chapter 5, "A Dwarf Planet"

Mark each statement *T* for true or *F* for false.

_F_ 1. The Milky Way contains nine planets.
_T_ 2. When scientists learned more about Pluto, they decided it was not the same as the other planets.
_T_ 3. Pluto may have been one of Neptune's moons.
_T_ 4. Pluto is now called a dwarf planet.
_F_ 5. Pluto is the closest planet to Earth.
_T_ 6. It takes nine years to go from Earth to Pluto.
_F_ 7. The students were much heavier on Pluto than on Earth.
_T_ 8. The class needed space suits and helmets to go onto Pluto.
_F_ 9. The students were eager to go home.
_F_ 10. Simon clicked on the last link—*Home.*

Read the question, and write your answer.

Why were the students able to pick each other up so easily on Pluto?
Pluto is very small so the pull of gravity is weak. That makes
everything much lighter there than it is on Earth.

30   Anything's Possible • Book 2

Hyperlinking through the Solar System

Chapter Quiz

Name _____ **Date** _____

Hyperlinking through the Solar System
Chapter 6, "The Journey Ends"

Number the events in order from 1 to 5.

_3_ A comet passed the rocket.
_5_ The students were back in the computer lab.
_2_ The rocket left Pluto.
_4_ Dr. Sanchez pressed a button on the computer and there was a sudden flash of light.
_1_ The students took off their space suits and sat down.

Mark each statement *T* for true or *F* for false.

_T_ 1. A comet contains frozen ice, gases, and dust.
_F_ 2. A comet orbits the planet it is closest to.
_T_ 3. Mr. Todd does odd things sometimes.
_F_ 4. The students needed to wear space suits in the rocket ship.

Read the question, and write your answer.

Why do you think the author used fiction and nonfiction together in this story?
Reasonable answers should recognize that the fiction aspect
makes the learning of the scientific facts more interesting.

Anything's Possible • Book 2   31

Hyperlinking through the Solar System

Thinking and Writing

Name _____ **Date** _____

Hyperlinking through the Solar System
Think About It

Write about or give an oral presentation for each question.

1. How can you explore the galaxy using hyperlinks?
   There are many useful Web sites, from NASA to universities
   to planetariums. By visiting these Web sites and using the
   hyperlinks contained in each, you can explore the galaxy virtually.

2. How would gravity on Jupiter compare to gravity on Pluto?
   Jupiter is the biggest planet and Pluto is a dwarf planet. This
   means there is more gravity on Jupiter, so items are heavier
   on Jupiter than on Pluto.

3. How are the asteroid belt, the rings of Saturn, and a comet similar?
   None of them are solid. All three are made of larger and
   smaller pieces.

Write About It

Choose one of the questions below. Write your answer on a sheet of paper.

1. If you could explore our solar system, where would you go? Write a letter to a friend telling where you would want to explore and what you would want to learn.

2. Imagine you are an astronomer from 1650 and you have just been transported to the present time. You spent the day at a planetarium studying the rings of Saturn with a NASA astronomer. Write a one-page diary entry telling about what you learned and why you didn't know that in 1650.

3. Complete the Genres Chart for this book.

32   Anything's Possible • Book 2

Hyperlinking through the Solar System

Name _____ Date _____

Seven Wonders of the World
What You Know

Write answers to these questions.

1. What is a skyscraper? How are they built today?

_____

_____

2. Use an atlas to find the following: China, Jordan, Cambodia, India, Peru, Easter Island, and Brazil. List each country and the continent or area where it is found.

_____

_____

3. What is a wonder? Why would people consider a building a wonder?

_____

_____

Word Meanings
Matching

Look for these words as you read your chapter book. When you find a word, draw a line to connect the word with the correct definition.

swamp   a hard, stony substance

shrine   a sculptured or ornamental band

wonder   a building or place for worship

frieze   a piece of wet, spongy land

coral   something unusual and amazing

Seven Wonders of the World

Unfamiliar Words	Word Meanings	Proper Nouns	
build, gems, god, goddess, wonderful, world	wonder	The Colossus of Rhodes, Egypt, The Hanging Gardens of Babylon, King Croesus, The Pharos of Alexandria, The Great Pyramid of Giza, The Statue of Zeus, The Temple of Artemis, The Mausoleum at Halicarnassus	**Chapter 1**
cannons, emperor, fighting, towers	swamp	The Great Wall of China	**Chapter 2**
built, city, desert, jungle, mountain, once	frieze	Angkor Wat, Cambodia, Greece, India, Jordan, Nabatea, Petra, Roman Empire, Switzerland	**Chapter 3**
married, pictures	shrine	Agra, Shah Jahan, Taj Mahal	**Chapter 4**
faces, flew, huge, remote, spaceships	coral	Easter Island, Nazca, Pacific Ocean, Peru	**Chapter 5**
		Brasilia, Brazil	**Chapter 6**

Name _____ Date _____

Seven Wonders of the World
Chapter 1, "Wonders of Long Ago"

Fill in the bubble beside the answer for each question.

1. Both the Great Pyramid of Giza and the Mausoleum at Halicarnassus were

    Ⓐ temples.

    Ⓑ tombs.

    Ⓒ both A and B

2. The Colossus of Rhodes was

    Ⓐ a huge statue.

    Ⓑ a lighthouse.

    Ⓒ a temple.

3. The Hanging Gardens of Babylon were

    Ⓐ trees and flowers planted on the roofs of houses.

    Ⓑ planted without dirt.

    Ⓒ both A and B

4. The Pharos of Alexandria was

    Ⓐ a statue covered in gold and gems.

    Ⓑ built by King Croesus.

    Ⓒ a lighthouse.

Read the question, and write your answer.

Which of the Seven Wonders of the World do you think was the most difficult to build? Explain your answer.

_____

_____

Name _____ Date _____

Seven Wonders of the World
Chapter 2, "The Great Wall of China"

Number the events in order from 1 to 5.

_____ The work on the wall took hundreds of years.

_____ China could not keep enemies out.

_____ All of China was walled off.

_____ The emperor of China had a plan to keep enemies out.

_____ Parts of the wall fell down.

Mark each statement _T_ for true or _F_ for false.

_____   **1.** The Great Wall of China was over 4,000 miles long.

_____   **2.** People could climb over the wall.

_____   **3.** The wall had towers and a footpath on top.

_____   **4.** If a guard saw an enemy, he would blow a trumpet for help.

Read the question, and write your answer.

What were some of the difficulties faced by workers on the Great Wall
of China?

_____

_____

_____

_____

Name _____ Date _____

Seven Wonders of the World
Chapter 3, "Petra and Angkor Wat"

Number the events in order from 1 to 5.

_____ Nabateans carved a city from sandstone.

_____ The "lost" city was found by a man from Switzerland.

_____ Petra became a rich and busy city.

_____ Traders began using Roman roads instead of the Petra road.

_____ Traders needed a place in the desert to rest and eat.

Number the events in order from 6 to 10.

_____ The king of Angkor died.

_____ Angkor became the home of monkeys and rats.

_____ Miles of jungle were cleared to build Angkor.

_____ Angkor fell to enemies, and the people left.

_____ Angkor was beautiful, with statues, homes, and temples.

Read the question, and write your answer.

Compare the reasons people left Petra with the reasons people left Angkor.

_____

_____

_____

Name _____ Date _____

Seven Wonders of the World
Chapter 4, "The Taj Mahal"

Fill in the bubble beside the answer for each question.

1. The Taj Mahal was built in
   Ⓐ India.
   Ⓑ Cambodia.
   Ⓒ Jordan.

2. Shah Jahan built the Taj Mahal as a tomb for
   Ⓐ his children.
   Ⓑ his wife.
   Ⓒ himself.

3. To build the Taj Mahal, Shah Jahan used
   Ⓐ all the best workers and artists.
   Ⓑ as much money as needed to make the building wonderful.
   Ⓒ both A and B

4. Shah Jahan wanted the Taj Mahal to
   Ⓐ be the biggest building in the world.
   Ⓑ be very beautiful.
   Ⓒ last forever.

Read the question, and write your answer.

What else did Shah Jahan build at Agra besides the Taj Mahal?

_____

_____

_____

Name _____ Date _____

Seven Wonders of the World
Chapter 5, "Nazca and Easter Island"

Mark each statement *T* for true or *F* for false.

_____ **1.** Some people believe the lines of Nazca were built by people from space.

_____ **2.** Nazca is in Chile.

_____ **3.** The pictures and lines can be seen best from the air.

_____ **4.** The pictures were made by placing millions of small rocks on the ground.

_____ **5.** The people of Nazca made the pictures 1,500 years ago.

_____ **6.** The statues on Easter Island are like the statues in Egypt.

_____ **7.** Easter Island is in the Indian Ocean.

_____ **8.** Hundreds of huge statues ring Easter Island.

_____ **9.** The statues were carved on the island's rock walls and moved to flat sites.

_____ **10.** The only tools used were bone picks and small wooden sticks.

Read the question, and write your answer.

Why are the pictures and lines of Nazca a wonder?

_____

_____

_____

_____

Name _____ Date _____

Seven Wonders of the World
Chapter 6, "Brasilia—A Wonder?"

Number the events in order from 1 to 5.

____ Airplanes flew in tools and food.

____ An airplane landing strip was made in the jungle.

____ In 1960 the city opened.

____ Brazil wanted a new capital city.

____ The new highways and cars were bad for the jungle.

Mark each statement *T* for true or *F* for false.

____ 1. Brazil built a capital city on the ruins of an old town.

____ 2. The city was built in the middle of the country.

____ 3. Mold grows in the city because of the damp jungle air.

____ 4. It costs a lot of money to take care of Brasilia.

Read the question, and write your answer.

Why do people say that Brasilia should have been planned better?

_____

_____

_____

_____

Name _____ Date _____

Seven Wonders of the World
Think About It

Write about or give an oral presentation for each question.

1. Which of the wonders described in this book do you think is most
    wonderful? Why?

    _____

    _____

2. Compare the building and cost of taking care of the Great Wall of China
    with that of the city of Brasilia. What do you think will happen to Brasilia?

    _____

    _____

3. If the statues on Easter Island were built today, what would be
    different in how they were made? Would they still be wonders?

    _____

    _____

    _____

Write About It

**Choose one of the questions below. Write your answer on a sheet
of paper.**

1. Imagine you are a travel agent. Write an advertisement for a tour
    of the seven wonders described in Chapters 2 through 6. What will
    people see? Why should they visit these wonders?

2. Pretend you are the last person in Petra. Write a letter to leave
    behind when you go away. In your letter tell why Petra was built,
    what it was like in the rich years, and why everyone left.

3. Complete the Timeline for this book.

Seven Wonders of the World

Chapter 2 *pages 6 and 7*

*The wall went up high hills, across rushing streams, and through wet	12
swamps. There were few towns along the way. The work went on for	25
hundreds of years.	28

The wall had big stones on the outside and rocks or sand inside. On	42
top were towers to hide behind. There was a wide footpath on top so the	57
army could patrol the wall. If anyone saw an enemy, he would light a fire	72
on a tower. Armed men would come running when they saw the fire. Later	86
the wall was lined* with cannons.	92

By the early 1600s all of China was walled off.	102

Chapter 3 *page 11*

*How could so many people live in the desert? The Nabateans were	12
very smart. They made dams and pipes to bring water from the mountain.	25
There was lots of water for growing food and for drinking. Better still,	38
Petra was safe. The only way to Petra was through a small opening between	52
two high walls. No army could rush through.	60

All went well until the Roman Empire took over around A.D. 100. The	73
Romans made fine roads everywhere. Traders stopped using the Petra road.	84
Their tax money went with them.* Everyone left the city. After hundreds of	97
years, people forgot it was there.	103

- The target rate for **Anything's Possible** is 90 wcpm. The asterisks (*) mark 90 words.

- Listen to the student read the passage. Count the number of words read in one minute and the number of errors.

- For the reading rate, subtract the number of errors from the total number of words read.

- Have students enter their scores on their **Fluency Graph.** See page 9.

Building Background

Name _____ Date _____

Seven Wonders of the World
What You Know
Write answers to these questions.

1. What is a skyscraper? How are they built today?
   tall building with many floors; with huge machines,
   high-powered tools, and a variety of materials

2. Use an atlas to find the following: China, Jordan, Cambodia, India, Peru, Easter Island, and Brazil. List each country and the continent or area where it is found.
   China, Asia; Jordan, Middle East; Cambodia, Asia; India, Asia; Peru,
   South America; Easter Island, Pacific Ocean off South America; Brazil,
   South America

3. What is a wonder? Why would people consider a building a wonder?
   A wonder is something really unusual; answers may include
   size, shape, or expense.

Word Meanings
Matching

Look for these words as you read your chapter book. When you find a word, draw a line to connect the word with the correct definition.

swamp — a hard, stony substance
shrine — a sculptured or ornamental band
wonder — a building or place for worship
frieze — a piece of wet, spongy land
coral — something unusual and amazing

36 Anything's Possible • Book 3

Seven Wonders of the World

Chapter Quiz

Name _____ Date _____

Seven Wonders of the World
Chapter 1, "Wonders of Long Ago"
Fill in the bubble beside the answer for each question.

1. Both the Great Pyramid of Giza and the Mausoleum at Halicarnassus were
   Ⓐ temples.
   ● tombs.
   Ⓒ both A and B

2. The Colossus of Rhodes was
   ● a huge statue.
   Ⓑ a lighthouse.
   Ⓒ a temple.

3. The Hanging Gardens of Babylon were
   Ⓐ trees and flowers planted on the roofs of houses.
   Ⓑ planted without dirt.
   ● both A and B

4. The Pharos of Alexandria was
   Ⓐ a statue covered in gold and gems.
   Ⓑ built by King Croesus.
   ● a lighthouse.

Read the question, and write your answer.

Which of the Seven Wonders of the World do you think was the most difficult to build? Explain your answer.
Accept reasonable responses.

38 Anything's Possible • Book 3

Seven Wonders of the World

Chapter Quiz

Name _____ Date _____

Seven Wonders of the World
Chapter 2, "The Great Wall of China"
Number the events in order from 1 to 5.

 3 The work on the wall took hundreds of years.
 1 China could not keep enemies out.
 4 All of China was walled off.
 2 The emperor of China had a plan to keep enemies out.
 5 Parts of the wall fell down.

Mark each statement *T* for true or *F* for false.

 T 1. The Great Wall of China was over 4,000 miles long.
 F 2. People could climb over the wall.
 T 3. The wall had towers and a footpath on top.
 F 4. If a guard saw an enemy, he would blow a trumpet for help.

Read the question, and write your answer.

What were some of the difficulties faced by workers on the Great Wall of China?
Ideas: had to carry stones on their backs for miles; worked
in heat, rain, and snow; built the wall over high hills, across
streams, and through swamps; there were few towns along
the way

Anything's Possible • Book 3 39

Seven Wonders of the World

Chapter Quiz

Name _____ Date _____

Seven Wonders of the World
Chapter 3, "Petra and Angkor Wat"
Number the events in order from 1 to 5.

 2 Nabateans carved a city from sandstone.
 5 The "lost" city was found by a man from Switzerland.
 3 Petra became a rich and busy city.
 4 Traders began using Roman roads instead of the Petra road.
 1 Traders needed a place in the desert to rest and eat.

Number the events in order from 6 to 10.

 8 The king of Angkor died.
10 Angkor became the home of monkeys and rats.
 6 Miles of jungle were cleared to build Angkor.
 9 Angkor fell to enemies, and the people left.
 7 Angkor was beautiful, with statues, homes, and temples.

Read the question, and write your answer.

Compare the reasons people left Petra with the reasons people left Angkor.
People left Petra because the Petra road was no longer used,
so tax money stopped coming in; people left Angkor because
the city was taken over by enemies.

40 Anything's Possible • Book 3

Seven Wonders of the World

Name _____ Date _____

Seven Wonders of the World
Chapter 4, "The Taj Mahal"
Fill in the bubble beside the answer for each question.

1. The Taj Mahal was built in
   ● India.
   Ⓑ Cambodia.
   Ⓒ Jordan.

2. Shah Jahan built the Taj Mahal as a tomb for
   Ⓐ his children.
   ● his wife.
   Ⓒ himself.

3. To build the Taj Mahal, Shah Jahan used
   Ⓐ all the best workers and artists.
   Ⓑ as much money as needed to make the building wonderful.
   ● both A and B

4. Shah Jahan wanted the Taj Mahal to
   Ⓐ be the biggest building in the world.
   ● be very beautiful.
   Ⓒ last forever.

Read the question, and write your answer.

What else did Shah Jahan build at Agra besides the Taj Mahal?
a gateway, a garden, a temple, and a rest house

Name _____ Date _____

Seven Wonders of the World
Chapter 5, "Nazca and Easter Island"
Mark each statement *T* for true or *F* for false.

_T_ 1. Some people believe the lines of Nazca were built by people from space.

_F_ 2. Nazca is in Chile.

_T_ 3. The pictures and lines can be seen best from the air.

_T_ 4. The pictures were made by placing millions of small rocks on the ground.

_F_ 5. The people of Nazca made the pictures 1,500 years ago.

_F_ 6. The statues on Easter Island are like the statues in Egypt.

_F_ 7. Easter Island is in the Indian Ocean.

_T_ 8. Hundreds of huge statues ring Easter Island.

_T_ 9. The statues were carved on the island's rock walls and moved to flat sites.

_F_ 10. The only tools used were bone picks and small wooden sticks.

Read the question, and write your answer.

Why are the pictures and lines of Nazca a wonder?
They are made up of millions of small rocks, and designs are
so big it is hard to see what they are from the ground. They
are best seen from the air, and people didn't have airplanes
2,000 years ago.

Name _____ Date _____

Seven Wonders of the World
Chapter 6, "Brasilia—A Wonder?"
Number the events in order from 1 to 5.

_3_ Airplanes flew in tools and food.

_2_ An airplane landing strip was made in the jungle.

_4_ In 1960 the city opened.

_1_ Brazil wanted a new capital city.

_5_ The new highways and cars were bad for the jungle.

Mark each statement *T* for true or *F* for false.

_F_ 1. Brazil built a capital city on the ruins of an old town.

_T_ 2. The city was built in the middle of the country.

_T_ 3. Mold grows in the city because of the damp jungle air.

_T_ 4. It costs a lot of money to take care of Brasilia.

Read the question, and write your answer.

Why do people say that Brasilia should have been planned better?
Ideas: costs a lot of money care for the city; soft ground makes
streets and sidewalks crack; damp jungle air makes mold form
on buildings; lake is dirty; highways and cars are bad for jungle
plants and animals

Name _____ Date _____

Seven Wonders of the World
Think About It
Write about or give an oral presentation for each question.

1. Which of the wonders described in this book do you think is most wonderful? Why?
   Answers will vary.

2. Compare the building and cost of taking care of the Great Wall of China with that of the city of Brasilia. What do you think will happen to Brasilia?
   Answers will vary.

3. If the statues on Easter Island were built today, what would be different in how they were made? Would they still be wonders?
   Advanced technology and tools would be used; limited tools
   available to construct, move, and set up the huge statues is
   part of their wonder.

Write About It
Choose one of the questions below. Write your answer on a sheet of paper.

1. Imagine you are a travel agent. Write an advertisement for a tour of the seven wonders described in Chapters 2 through 6. What will people see? Why should they visit these wonders?

2. Pretend you are the last person in Petra. Write a letter to leave behind when you go away. In your letter tell why Petra was built, what it was like in the rich years, and why everyone left.

3. Complete the Timeline for this book.

Name _____ Date _____

Race to Space
What You Know

Write answers to these questions.

1. Conduct research and list some ways the Cold War helped motivate the space race.

   _____

   _____

2. Would you like to travel in space? Why or why not?

   _____

   _____

3. What is the difference between competition and cooperation? Give an example of each.

   _____

   _____

Word Meanings
Definitions

Look for these words as you read your chapter book. When you find one of these words, write its definition.

cosmonaut: _____

decade: _____

parachute: _____

satellite: _____

space: _____

splashdown: _____

Race to Space

Chapter	Unfamiliar Words	Word Meanings	Proper Nouns
Chapter 1	dreamed enemies fighting mysteries mystery possible race	space	Soviet Union United States World War II
Chapter 2	control died fuel launch secret	satellite	Explorer *Sputnik*
Chapter 3	astronauts capsule chief countries decision designer module problems program spacecraft	cosmonaut	Germany Project Mercury Russian *Vostok* Wernher von Braun
Chapter 4	aircraft flew knew navy western	parachute	Alan Shepard Jr. New Hampshire Yuri Gagarin
Chapter 5	different minute worry	splashdown	Atlantic Ocean *Freedom 7* Moscow
Chapter 6	choose scientists	decade	*Apollo 14* *International Space Station* John F. Kennedy Russia Sergei Korolev

Name _____ Date _____

Race to Space
Chapter 1, "The Space Race"

Fill in the bubble beside the answer for each question.

1. Why did people dream about flying into space?
   - Ⓐ They liked to fly in rockets and jets.
   - Ⓑ They wanted to win the space race.
   - Ⓒ They wanted to find the answer to the mystery of the sky.

2. When did flying to space become possible?
   - Ⓐ at the end of the Cold War
   - Ⓑ after World War II
   - Ⓒ during World War II

3. Why did the United States and the Soviet Union become enemies after World War II?
   - Ⓐ They did not think about things the same way, and they did not trust each other.
   - Ⓑ They each wanted to take over the world.
   - Ⓒ They each wanted to get to space first.

4. What did the United States and the Soviet Union begin making in order to take the Cold War into space?
   - Ⓐ bigger planes
   - Ⓑ bigger rockets
   - Ⓒ flying saucers

Read the question, and write your answer.

Why did going into space seem possible at the end of World War II?

_____

_____

Name _____ Date _____

Race to Space
Chapter 2, *"Sputnik"*

Mark each statement *T* for true or *F* for false.

_____ 1. The first step into space was a satellite.

_____ 2. The United States and the Soviet Union wanted to spy on each other using satellites.

_____ 3. The United States knew all about the Soviet space program.

_____ 4. *Sputnik* was launched in 1961.

_____ 5. A rocket carried *Sputnik* into space.

_____ 6. *Sputnik* never made it into space.

_____ 7. *Sputnik's* blinking light could be seen in the night sky.

_____ 8. *Sputnik* carried a human into space.

_____ 9. The United States was beating the Soviet Union in the space race.

_____ 10. The United States launched its first satellite in 1960.

Read the question, and write your answer.

Why did most people in the United States think the Soviet Union could not launch a satellite?

_____

_____

_____

Name _____ Date _____

Race to Space
Chapter 3, "Mercury and Vostok"

Number the events in order from 1 to 5.

____ Both the Soviet Union's and the United States' teams decided a capsule would carry people into space.

____ Wernher Von Braun came to the United States.

____ Teams made different designs for spacecraft, including one for a space plane.

____ Von Braun designed rockets for Germany.

____ The Soviet team made a small capsule.

Number the events in order from 6 to 10.

____ Von Braun decided to be safe and test the spacecraft once more.

____ The United States' space program decided to test space flight on a chimp before allowing astronauts to go to space.

____ The United States chose March 24, 1961, as the day the first astronaut would go into space.

____ A body made of rubber flew in the space capsule.

____ A chimp named Ham went up and down in the capsule.

Read the question, and write your answer.

Why do you think both the United States and the Soviet Union chose the capsule design for their spacecraft?

_____

_____

Name _____ Date _____

Race to Space
Chapter 4, "Gagarin and Shepard"

Mark each statement *T* for true or *F* for false.

____ 1. The letter that went to the Soviet flight school asked, "Who wants to be an airline pilot?"

____ 2. The Soviets chose ten pilots to train to be cosmonauts.

____ 3. Yuri Gagarin was small and thin.

____ 4. To train to be a cosmonaut, Gagarin flew jets, practiced parachuting, and ran for miles.

____ 5. During their training, the cosmonauts did not see *Vostok*.

____ 6. Alan Shepard served in the navy during World War II.

____ 7. Shepard was too shy to show off his flying skills.

____ 8. Test pilots fly higher and faster than anyone else.

____ 9. The first group of astronauts was called the *Mercury Five*.

____ 10. Shepard was chosen to be the first person in space.

Read the question, and write your answer.

How were Gagarin and Shepard alike? How were they different?

_____

_____

_____

_____

Name _____ Date _____

Race to Space
Chapter 5, "Liftoff!"

Number the events in order from 1 to 5.

_____ Parachutes on *Freedom 7* opened, and it landed in the
Atlantic Ocean.

_____ On April 12, 1961, Gagarin became the first person to go into space.

_____ Shepard went into space in *Freedom 7*.

_____ Gagarin landed on a farm.

_____ The chief designer picked Gagarin to be the first cosmonaut
in space.

Mark each statement *T* for true or *F* for false.

_____ **1.** The chief designer chose Gagarin to be the first cosmonaut in
space without talking with him.

_____ **2.** Gagarin was able to control the space capsule as it orbited
around Earth.

_____ **3.** *Freedom 7* moved at 5,000 miles per hour.

_____ **4.** Shepard could move the spacecraft up, down, left, and right.

Read the question, and write your answer.

Why was Shepard upset and sad when he heard about *Vostok*?

_____

_____

_____

Name _____ Date _____

Race to Space
Chapter 6, "Next Stop: The Moon"

Fill in the bubble beside the answer for each question.

1. Who said, "We choose to go to the moon in this decade and do the other things, not because they are easy, but because they are hard . . . ."?
   Ⓐ Wernher von Braun
   Ⓑ John F. Kennedy
   Ⓒ Alan Shepard

2. What was the name of the Soviet Union's chief designer?
   Ⓐ Sergei Korolev
   Ⓑ Wernher von Braun
   Ⓒ Yuri Gagarin

3. In what year did an American astronaut first land on the moon?
   Ⓐ 1968
   Ⓑ 1971
   Ⓒ 1969

4. Who works on the *International Space Station?*
   Ⓐ the *Apollo* team
   Ⓑ scientists from many countries around the world
   Ⓒ only cosmonauts

Read the question, and write your answer.

Why did the space race become history?

_____

_____

_____

Name _____ Date _____

Race to Space
Think About It

Write about or give an oral presentation for each question.

1. Describe Gagarin and Shepard. Why do you think these two men were chosen to be the first people in space?

    _____

2. Why would the Soviets keep their space program secret?

    _____

3. President Kennedy said, "We choose to go to the moon in this decade and do the other things, not because they are easy, but because they are hard . . . ." Why was it hard to go to the moon?

    _____

4. Today the space race is history, but people still go to space and study it. Is the study of space more or less interesting now that there is no longer a race? Why?

    _____

Write About It

Choose one of the questions below. Write your answer on a sheet of paper.

1. Pretend you are Shepard. You have just been told that you will be the first American in space. Write a letter to your best friend to tell him or her the exciting news. Tell your friend how you have been training to go to space and what you will do in space.

2. The first astronauts and cosmonauts took many risks when they took part in the race to space. People going to space still take risks today. Are the risks worth it? Why or why not?

3. Complete the Sequencing Chart for this book.

Race to Space

Chapter 2 *page 5*

*The launch of *Sputnik* scared many people. Its blinking light could be	12
seen in the night sky. Would the Soviet Union take control of space?	25

The Soviet people were very proud of *Sputnik*. Millions of Soviet	36
people had died in World War II. Their factories had been burned. Few	49
could find food to eat. But now their country was beating the United States	63
in the space race.	67

The launch of *Sputnik* made the United States work faster. In January	79
1958 the United States launched its first satellite. It was called* *Explorer*.	91
Now there was a new question. Who would send a person into space first?	105

Chapter 5 *page 19*

**Vostok* flew 200 miles high. Then it went into orbit around Earth.	12
Gagarin did not control the capsule, the module did. The capsule was	24
moving thousands of miles an hour. Gagarin looked out the window. He	36
was the first person to see Earth from space.	45

Vostok went almost all the way around Earth. After 78 minutes, the	57
capsule came away from the module. Then the capsule started falling back	69
to Earth. It fell four miles a minute.	77

Then the capsule's door came off. Gagarin got out of the capsule. He*	90
was more than four miles away from the ground. He opened his parachute.	103

- The target rate for **Anything's Possible** is 90 wcpm. The asterisks (*) mark 90 words.

- Listen to the student read the passage. Count the number of words read in one minute and the number of errors.

- For the reading rate, subtract the number of errors from the total number of words read.

- Have students enter their scores on their **Fluency Graph.** See page 9.

Answer Key

Name _____ Date _____

Race to Space
What You Know

Write answers to these questions.

1. Conduct research and list some ways the Cold War helped motivate the space race.
   Accept reasonable responses.
   _____

2. Would you like to travel in space? Why or why not?
   Accept reasonable responses.
   _____

3. What is the difference between competition and cooperation? Give an example of each.
   Competition **is when people try to discover who is best at**
   something. ***Cooperation*** **is when people work together to get**
   something done. Accept reasonable examples.

Word Meanings
Definitions

Look for these words as you read your chapter book. When you find one of these words, write its definition.

cosmonaut: **a Soviet or Russian astronaut**

decade: **a period of ten years**

parachute: **a large cloth device that opens up like an umbrella and is used to slow down a person dropping from a great height**

satellite: **a moon or a man-made object that orbits around a planet**

space: **the area that stretches in all directions, has no limits, and contains all things in the universe**

splashdown: **the landing of a spacecraft in the ocean**

48   Anything's Possible • Book 4

Race to Space

Name _____ Date _____

Race to Space
Chapter 1, "The Space Race"

Fill in the bubble beside the answer for each question.

1. Why did people dream about flying into space?
   - (A) They liked to fly in rockets and jets.
   - (B) They wanted to win the space race.
   - ● They wanted to find the answer to the mystery of the sky.

2. When did flying to space become possible?
   - (A) at the end of the Cold War
   - ● after World War II
   - (C) during World War II

3. Why did the United States and the Soviet Union become enemies after World War II?
   - ● They did not think about things the same way, and they did not trust each other.
   - (B) They each wanted to take over the world.
   - (C) They each wanted to get to space first.

4. What did the United States and the Soviet Union begin making in order to take the Cold War into space?
   - (A) bigger planes
   - ● bigger rockets
   - (C) flying saucers

Read the question, and write your answer.

Why did going into space seem possible at the end of World War II?
The Soviet Union and the United States began making bigger
rockets that could fly higher than ever before.

50   Anything's Possible • Book 4

Race to Space

Name _____ Date _____

Race to Space
Chapter 2, "Sputnik"

Mark each statement *T* for true or *F* for false.

- **T** 1. The first step into space was a satellite.
- **T** 2. The United States and the Soviet Union wanted to spy on each other using satellites.
- **F** 3. The United States knew all about the Soviet space program.
- **F** 4. *Sputnik* was launched in 1961.
- **T** 5. A rocket carried *Sputnik* into space.
- **F** 6. *Sputnik* never made it into space.
- **T** 7. *Sputnik's* blinking light could be seen in the night sky.
- **F** 8. *Sputnik* carried a human into space.
- **F** 9. The United States was beating the Soviet Union in the space race.
- **F** 10. The United States launched its first satellite in 1960.

Read the question, and write your answer.

Why did most people in the United States think the Soviet Union could not launch a satellite?
The United States did not know what the Soviet Union was
doing. The Soviets kept their space program secret.

Anything's Possible • Book 4   51

Race to Space

Name _____ Date _____

Race to Space
Chapter 3, "Mercury and Vostok"

Number the events in order from 1 to 5.

- **4** Both the Soviet Union's and the United States' teams decided a capsule would carry people into space.
- **2** Wernher Von Braun came to the United States.
- **3** Teams made different designs for spacecraft, including one for a space plane.
- **1** Von Braun designed rockets for Germany.
- **5** The Soviet team made a small capsule.

Number the events in order from 6 to 10.

- **9** Von Braun decided to be safe and test the spacecraft once more.
- **7** The United States' space program decided to test space flight on a chimp before allowing astronauts to go to space.
- **6** The United States chose March 24, 1961, as the day the first astronaut would go into space.
- **10** A body made of rubber flew in the space capsule.
- **8** A chimp named Ham went up and down in the capsule.

Read the question, and write your answer.

Why do you think both the United States and the Soviet Union chose the capsule design for their spacecraft?
It was easier than other ideas like the space plane. It would be
just like a satellite.

52   Anything's Possible • Book 4

Race to Space

58   **Anything's Possible • Book 4**

Chapter Quiz

Name _____ Date _____

Race to Space
Chapter 4, "Gagarin and Shepard"

Mark each statement *T* for true or *F* for false.

_F_ 1. The letter that went to the Soviet flight school asked, "Who wants to be an airline pilot?"

_F_ 2. The Soviets chose ten pilots to train to be cosmonauts.

_T_ 3. Yuri Gagarin was small and thin.

_T_ 4. To train to be a cosmonaut, Gagarin flew jets, practiced parachuting, and ran for miles.

_T_ 5. During their training, the cosmonauts did not see *Vostok*.

_T_ 6. Alan Shepard served in the navy during World War II.

_F_ 7. Shepard was too shy to show off his flying skills.

_T_ 8. Test pilots fly higher and faster than anyone else.

_F_ 9. The first group of astronauts was called the *Mercury Five*.

_T_ 10. Shepard was chosen to be the first person in space.

Read the question, and write your answer.

How were Gagarin and Shepard alike? How were they different?
Both were pilots, and both were chosen to be the first person
in space for their countries. Gagarin was from the Soviet Union
and Shepard was from the United States. Gagarin was a boy
in World War II. Shepard fought in World War II.

Race to Space

Chapter Quiz

Name _____ Date _____

Race to Space
Chapter 5, "Liftoff!"

Number the events in order from 1 to 5.

_5_ Parachutes on *Freedom 7* opened, and it landed in the Atlantic Ocean.

_2_ On April 12, 1961, Gagarin became the first person to go into space.

_4_ Shepard went into space in *Freedom 7*.

_3_ Gagarin landed on a farm.

_1_ The chief designer picked Gagarin to be the first cosmonaut in space.

Mark each statement *T* for true or *F* for false.

_F_ 1. The chief designer chose Gagarin to be the first cosmonaut in space without talking with him.

_F_ 2. Gagarin was able to control the space capsule as it orbited around Earth.

_T_ 3. *Freedom 7* moved at 5,000 miles per hour.

_T_ 4. Shepard could move the spacecraft up, down, left, and right.

Read the question, and write your answer.

Why was Shepard upset and sad when he heard about *Vostok*?
He had wanted to be the first person in space. The United
States was still behind in the space race.

Race to Space

Chapter Quiz

Name _____ Date _____

Race to Space
Chapter 6, "Next Stop: The Moon"

Fill in the bubble beside the answer for each question.

1. Who said, "We choose to go to the moon in this decade and do the other things, not because they are easy, but because they are hard . . . ."?
   - Ⓐ Wernher von Braun
   - ● John F. Kennedy
   - Ⓒ Alan Shepard

2. What was the name of the Soviet Union's chief designer?
   - ● Sergei Korolev
   - Ⓑ Wernher von Braun
   - Ⓒ Yuri Gagarin

3. In what year did an American astronaut first land on the moon?
   - Ⓐ 1968
   - Ⓑ 1971
   - ● 1969

4. Who works on the *International Space Station?*
   - Ⓐ the *Apollo* team
   - ● scientists from many countries around the world
   - Ⓒ only cosmonauts

Read the question, and write your answer.

Why did the space race become history?
The space race became history because countries started working
together on the *International Space Station*. They stopped competing
against each other and began cooperating with each other.

Race to Space

Thinking and Writing

Name _____ Date _____

Race to Space
Think About It

Write about or give an oral presentation for each question.

1. Describe Gagarin and Shepard. Why do you think these two men were chosen to be the first people in space? **Gagarin was small and would fit in the capsule. Shepard liked to show off. Both men wanted to go to space. They were good pilots, and they worked hard to learn about space travel.**

2. Why would the Soviets keep their space program secret? **Ideas: They wanted to beat the United States in the race to space. They were probably afraid if their program wasn't secret, other countries would spy on them and copy their ideas.**

3. President Kennedy said, "We choose to go to the moon in this decade and do the other things, not because they are easy, but because they are hard . . . ." Why was it hard to go to the moon? **Ideas: It was hard to go the moon because scientists had to make designs for spacecraft that would work and be safe. The astronauts had to be trained and tested to go to space. No one had ever done this before.**

4. Today the space race is history, but people still go to space and study it. Is the study of space more or less interesting now that there is no longer a race? Why?
   Accept reasonable responses.

Write About It

Choose one of the questions below. Write your answer on a sheet of paper.

1. Pretend you are Shepard. You have just been told that you will be the first American in space. Write a letter to your best friend to tell him or her the exciting news. Tell your friend how you have been training to go to space and what you will do in space.

2. The first astronauts and cosmonauts took many risks when they took part in the race to space. People going to space still take risks today. Are the risks worth it? Why or why not?

3. Complete the Sequencing Chart for this book.

Race to Space

Name _____ Date _____

Around the World
What You Know

Write answers to these questions.

1. List as many kinds of transportation, modern and old, as you can.

   _____

2. Pick two kinds of transportation that are used for long-distance travel. Compare and contrast them.

   _____

3. If you were to travel around the world, how would you do it? How long do you think the trip would take?

   _____

4. What would you take with you on a trip around the world? List up to five items, from most to least important.

   _____

Word Meanings
Matching

Look for these words as you read your chapter book. When you find a word, draw a line to connect the word with the correct definition.

goal   the person in charge of a ship

solar   something a person works toward

world   a contest to see who can go fastest

captain   depending on light or energy from the sun

race   what one thinks; an idea or opinion

thought   Earth

Around the World

	Unfamiliar Words	Word Meanings	Proper Nouns
Chapter 1	grew	world	Atlantic Ocean, Europe, Ferdinand Magellan, Pacific Ocean, Portugal, Spain, Spice Islands
Chapter 2	decided, husband, lonely	captain	Canada, England, Joshua Slocum, Lisa Clayton, Naomi James, New Zealand
Chapter 3	carried, flown, fuel, heavy, problem, propeller, record	race	Burt Rutan, California, Dick Rutan, Harold Gatty, Jeana Yeager, Los Angeles, New York City, Wiley Post
Chapter 4	catch, mountains, scientists, weather	thought	Bertrand Piccard, Brian Jones, France, Statue of Liberty
Chapter 5	adventure, amazing, breaking, knew	goal	Brazil, English Channel, Steve Fossett
Chapter 6	batteries, energy, enough, human, power	solar	Dave Kunst, Minnesota, Paris, United States, Expedition 360

Name _____ Date _____

Around the World
Chapter 1, "The First Trip"

Number the events in order from 1 to 5.

____ Ferdinand Magellan died before reaching the Spice Islands.

____ Magellan believed he could reach the Spice Islands by sailing west.

____ Magellan began his voyage in 1519 with five ships.

____ The king of Spain agreed to pay for Magellan's trip.

____ One ship and 18 sailors returned to Spain.

Mark each statement *T* for true or *F* for false.

____ 1. People in Europe used spices to make food taste better.

____ 2. Magellan's ships were the first to cross the Pacific Ocean.

____ 3. The sailors stayed healthy because they had good food to eat and clean water to drink.

____ 4. The voyage took five years.

Read the question, and write your answer.

Why is Magellan famous? _____

_____

_____

Name _____ Date _____

Around the World
Chapter 2, "Going It Alone"
Fill in the bubble beside the answer for each question.

1. When did the first person sail around the world alone?
   - Ⓐ in the 1900s
   - Ⓑ in the 1800s
   - Ⓒ in the 1700s

2. Who was the first person to sail around the world alone?
   - Ⓐ Ferdinand Magellan
   - Ⓑ Naomi James
   - Ⓒ Joshua Slocum

3. How long did it take James to sail around the world?
   - Ⓐ 272 days
   - Ⓑ over three years
   - Ⓒ 72 days

4. What was Clayton's goal?
   - Ⓐ to sail around the world faster than anyone else
   - Ⓑ to be the first woman to sail the world without stopping
   - Ⓒ to be the first woman to build her own boat and sail it around the world

Read the question, and write your answer.

Compare and contrast the voyages of Slocum and James.

_____

_____

_____

_____

Name _____ Date _____

Around the World
Chapter 3, "Flying High"

Number the events in order from 1 to 5.

_____ Wiley Post and Harold Gatty took off from New York City.

_____ Their plane was stuck in mud for 12 hours.

_____ Post wanted to be the first to fly around the world.

_____ The plane landed in New York City.

_____ The pilots stopped to get more fuel.

Number the events in order from 6 to 10.

_____ Jeana Yeager helped test the plane.

_____ After nine days, the plane landed in California.

_____ The Rutan brothers designed a plane that could fly around the world without stopping.

_____ Dick Rutan and Yeager took turns sleeping.

_____ Rutan and Yeager took off from California.

Read the question, and write your answer.

What qualities do you think test pilots need in order to succeed?

_____

_____

Name _____ Date _____

Around the World
Chapter 4, "Up, Up, and Away!"

Fill in the bubble beside the answer for each question.

1. What makes a hot-air balloon float?
   - Ⓐ gasoline-powered engines
   - Ⓑ wings on the sides of its basket
   - Ⓒ heated air

2. What did the first hot-air balloon do?
   - Ⓐ floated up in the sky
   - Ⓑ carried a duck, a sheep, and a chicken for two miles
   - Ⓒ stayed in the air for six days

3. Why does wind create problems for a hot-air balloon?
   - Ⓐ Wind can carry the balloon in a direction the rider does not want to go.
   - Ⓑ Wind can make balloons fly too high into the icy upper atmosphere.
   - Ⓒ Wind can make the hot air cold.

4. Which of the following is the most serious problem for travel in a hot-air balloon?
   - Ⓐ the threat of the basket catching on fire
   - Ⓑ storing sufficient supplies in the basket
   - Ⓒ bad weather

Read the question, and write your answer.

Why were Bertrand Piccard and Brian Jones able to sail around the world in a hot-air balloon when others had failed?

_____

_____

Name _____ Date _____

Around the World
Chapter 5, "Mr. Around-the-World"

Mark each statement *T* for true or *F* for false.

_____ **1.** Steve Fossett flew a plane around the world in less than three days.

_____ **2.** Fossett slept while the plane was on autopilot.

_____ **3.** Fossett made it around the world in a hot-air balloon the first time he tried.

_____ **4.** A fire broke out during Fossett's sixth hot-air balloon trip.

_____ **5.** It took 14 days for Fossett to travel around the world in a hot-air balloon.

_____ **6.** Fossett also traveled around the world in record time on a motor boat.

_____ **7.** Fossett always travels by himself.

_____ **8.** Although he has often flown over oceans, Fossett has never learned to swim.

_____ **9.** Fossett also races cars and climbs mountains.

_____ **10.** Fossett wants to fly a plane to where outer space begins.

Read the question, and write your answer.

Which of Fossett's adventures do you think was the most dangerous? Which do you think was most satisfying? Explain your answers.

_____

_____

Name _____ Date _____

Around the World
Chapter 6, "What's Next?"

Fill in the bubble beside the answer for each question.

1. How did Dave Kunst travel around the world?

   Ⓐ He flew in a hot-air balloon.

   Ⓑ He walked.

   Ⓒ He sailed in a small boat.

2. Expedition 360 members do which of these?

   Ⓐ travel on trips that last 360 days

   Ⓑ use "human power" to get around the world

   Ⓒ travel in groups of 360 people

3. The major problem facing solar planes is that

   Ⓐ the sun cannot power the plane batteries at night.

   Ⓑ the plane batteries are so heavy that the planes cannot fly at high altitudes.

   Ⓒ the planes are too small to carry people and their luggage.

4. Piccard hopes to make batteries that

   Ⓐ are small.

   Ⓑ are lightweight.

   Ⓒ store enough energy that a solar plane can fly at night.

Read the question, and write your answer.

What problems have the members of Expedition 360 faced during their trip?

_____

_____

Name _____ Date _____

Around the World
Think About It

Write about or give an oral presentation for each question.

1. Some of the men and women you read about traveled around the world in groups. Others traveled alone. Explain the challenges of each.

    _____

    _____

2. Rutan said, "If you can dream it, you can do it." What does he mean? Do you agree?

    _____

3. How do you think traveling around the world might change people? Explain your answer.

    _____

4. How are people who travel the globe today alike and different from explorers long ago?

    _____

    _____

Write About It

Choose one of the questions below. Write your answer on a sheet of paper.

1. Pretend you are the first person to travel around the globe. Write a letter to someone back home. Describe your transportation, what you see, and how you feel.

2. Choose one form of transportation described in this book. Write a checklist of everything the adventurer needed to make the trip a success.

3. Complete the Book Report Form for this book.

Around the World

Chapter 2 *page 5*

*One night robbers got onto his boat. But Slocum was ready. He had	13
put lots of tacks down. The robbers stepped on the tacks. They yelled in	27
pain and jumped into the sea.	33

Slocum was lonely sometimes. He got a goat for a pet. But it chomped	47
on his maps and his best hat. So he had to give the goat away at his next	65
stop. From then on, he talked to sea birds to cheer himself up.	78

It took Slocum more than three years to sail around the world.* He ran	92
into a bad storm as he neared home.	100

Chapter 5 *page 21*

*Fossett said he was lucky. But it was more than that. Fossett knew	13
what he was doing. He had been around the world two times before!	26

The first time was in 2002. He was in a hot-air balloon. He had tried	41
five times before to fly around the world in a hot-air balloon. But each time	56
something stopped him.	59

One time he crashed into a ranch in Brazil. Another time a storm	72
ripped open his balloon.	76

On his sixth try he made it. But even on that trip there were* problems.	91
A fire broke out. But Fossett put it out and kept going.	103

- The target rate for **Anything's Possible** is 90 wcpm. The asterisks (*) mark 90 words.

- Listen to the student read the passage. Count the number of words read in one minute and the number of errors.

- For the reading rate, subtract the number of errors from the total number of words read.

- Have students enter their scores on their **Fluency Graph.** See page 9.

Answer Key

Building Background

Name _____ Date _____

Around the World
What You Know

Write answers to these questions.

1. List as many kinds of transportation, modern and old, as you can.
   Ideas: cars, airplanes, buses, trains, boats, subways, bicycles, hot-air balloons, walking
2. Pick two kinds of transportation that are used for long-distance travel. Compare and contrast them.
   Accept reasonable responses.
3. If you were to travel around the world, how would you do it? How long do you think the trip would take?
   Accept reasonable responses.
4. What would you take with you on a trip around the world? List up to five items, from most to least important.
   Answers will vary, but ordering should show logic and reasoning.

Word Meanings
Matching

Look for these words as you read your chapter book. When you find a word, draw a line to connect the word with the correct definition.

goal — the person in charge of a ship
solar — something a person works toward
world — a contest to see who can go fastest
captain — depending on light or energy from the sun
race — what one thinks; an idea or opinion
thought — Earth

60   Anything's Possible • Book 5

Around the World

Chapter Quiz

Name _____ Date _____

Around the World
Chapter 1, "The First Trip"

Number the events in order from 1 to 5.

_4_ Ferdinand Magellan died before reaching the Spice Islands.
_1_ Magellan believed he could reach the Spice Islands by sailing west.
_3_ Magellan began his voyage in 1519 with five ships.
_2_ The king of Spain agreed to pay for Magellan's trip.
_5_ One ship and 18 sailors returned to Spain.

Mark each statement *T* for true or *F* for false.

_T_ 1. People in Europe used spices to make food taste better.
_T_ 2. Magellan's ships were the first to cross the Pacific Ocean.
_F_ 3. The sailors stayed healthy because they had good food to eat and clean water to drink.
_F_ 4. The voyage took five years.

Read the question, and write your answer.

Why is Magellan famous? _____
His ships were the first to sail across the Pacific Ocean; first to sail around the world; proved that the world was round.

62   Anything's Possible • Book 5

Around the World

Chapter Quiz

Name _____ Date _____

Around the World
Chapter 2, "Going It Alone"

Fill in the bubble beside the answer for each question.

1. When did the first person sail around the world alone?
   Ⓐ in the 1900s
   ● in the 1800s
   Ⓒ in the 1700s
2. Who was the first person to sail around the world alone?
   Ⓐ Ferdinand Magellan
   Ⓑ Naomi James
   ● Joshua Slocum
3. How long did it take James to sail around the world?
   ● 272 days
   Ⓑ over three years
   Ⓒ 72 days
4. What was Clayton's goal?
   Ⓐ to sail around the world faster than anyone else
   ● to be the first woman to sail the world without stopping
   Ⓒ to be the first woman to build her own boat and sail it around the world

Read the question, and write your answer.

Compare and contrast the voyages of Slocum and James.
Both sailed around the world alone, had animals for company, and faced challenges. Slocum was from Canada; James was from New Zealand. Slocum set out in 1895 and took more than three years. James set out in 1977 and took 272 days.

Anything's Possible • Book 5   63

Around the World

Chapter Quiz

Name _____ Date _____

Around the World
Chapter 3, "Flying High"

Number the events in order from 1 to 5.

_2_ Wiley Post and Harold Gatty took off from New York City.
_4_ Their plane was stuck in mud for 12 hours.
_1_ Post wanted to be the first to fly around the world.
_5_ The plane landed in New York City.
_3_ The pilots stopped to get more fuel.

Number the events in order from 6 to 10.

_7_ Jeana Yeager helped test the plane.
_10_ After nine days, the plane landed in California.
_6_ The Rutan brothers designed a plane that could fly around the world without stopping.
_9_ Dick Rutan and Yeager took turns sleeping.
_8_ Rutan and Yeager took off from California.

Read the question, and write your answer.

What qualities do you think test pilots need in order to succeed?
Ideas: patience; determination; good planning skills; the ability to work with others and to stay calm during emergencies

64   Anything's Possible • Book 5

Around the World

Name _____ Date _____

Around the World
Chapter 4, "Up, Up, and Away!"

Fill in the bubble beside the answer for each question.

1. What makes a hot-air balloon float?
   - Ⓐ gasoline-powered engines
   - Ⓑ wings on the sides of its basket
   - ● heated air

2. What did the first hot-air balloon do?
   - ● floated up in the sky
   - Ⓑ carried a duck, a sheep, and a chicken for two miles
   - Ⓒ stayed in the air for six days

3. Why does wind create problems for a hot-air balloon?
   - ● Wind can carry the balloon in a direction the rider does not want to go.
   - Ⓑ Wind can make balloons fly too high into the icy upper atmosphere.
   - Ⓒ Wind can make the hot air cold.

4. Which of the following is the most serious problem for travel in a hot-air balloon?
   - Ⓐ the threat of the basket catching on fire
   - Ⓑ storing sufficient supplies in the basket
   - ● bad weather

Read the question, and write your answer.

Why were Bertrand Piccard and Brian Jones able to sail around the world in a hot-air balloon when others had failed?

They used a bigger balloon; the wind helped carry them in the

right direction.

Name _____ Date _____

Around the World
Chapter 5, "Mr. Around-the-World"

Mark each statement *T* for true or *F* for false.

_T_ 1. Steve Fossett flew a plane around the world in less than three days.

_F_ 2. Fossett slept while the plane was on autopilot.

_F_ 3. Fossett made it around the world in a hot-air balloon the first time he tried.

_T_ 4. A fire broke out during Fossett's sixth hot-air balloon trip.

_T_ 5. It took 14 days for Fossett to travel around the world in a hot-air balloon.

_F_ 6. Fossett also traveled around the world in record time on a motor boat.

_F_ 7. Fossett always travels by himself.

_F_ 8. Although he has often flown over oceans, Fossett has never learned to swim.
T

____ 9. Fossett also races cars and climbs mountains.

_T_ 10. Fossett wants to fly a plane to where outer space begins.

Read the question, and write your answer.

Which of Fossett's adventures do you think was the most dangerous? Which do you think was most satisfying? Explain your answers.

Accept reasonable responses, but they should be supported

by information from the chapter.

Name _____ Date _____

Around the World
Chapter 6, "What's Next?"

Fill in the bubble beside the answer for each question.

1. How did Dave Kunst travel around the world?
   - Ⓐ He flew in a hot-air balloon.
   - ● He walked.
   - Ⓒ He sailed in a small boat.

2. Expedition 360 members do which of these?
   - Ⓐ travel on trips that last 360 days
   - ● use "human power" to get around the world
   - Ⓒ travel in groups of 360 people

3. The major problem facing solar planes is that
   - ● the sun cannot power the plane batteries at night.
   - Ⓑ the plane batteries are so heavy that the planes cannot fly at high altitudes.
   - Ⓒ the planes are too small to carry people and their luggage.

4. Piccard hopes to make batteries that
   - Ⓐ are small.
   - Ⓑ are lightweight.
   - ● store enough energy that a solar plane can fly at night.

Read the question, and write your answer.

What problems have the members of Expedition 360 faced during their trip?

Ideas: They were attacked by a shark; both of a team

member's legs were broken in a car accident.

Name _____ Date _____

Around the World
Think About It

Write about or give an oral presentation for each question.

1. Some of the men and women you read about traveled around the world in groups. Others traveled alone. Explain the challenges of each.
   Ideas: Traveling in a group means there are more people who can help, but requires cooperation, communication, and ability to get along with others. Traveling alone bestows a feeling of accomplishment with no help.

2. Rutan said, "If you can dream it, you can do it." What does he mean? Do you agree? **Ideas: If someone has an idea, he or she can make it happen. Many things can happen with hard work and determination.**

3. How do you think traveling around the world might change people? Explain your answer.
   Accept reasonable responses.

4. How are people who travel the globe today alike and different from explorers long ago?
   Explorers now have more choices for how to travel. Today, explorers might travel the globe to test new kinds of transportation or fuel, but long ago, explorers wanted to find new routes to faraway people and goods.

Write About It

Choose one of the questions below. Write your answer on a sheet of paper.

1. Pretend you are the first person to travel around the globe. Write a letter to someone back home. Describe your transportation, what you see, and how you feel.

2. Choose one form of transportation described in this book. Write a checklist of everything the adventurer needed to make the trip a success.

3. Complete the Book Report Form for this book.

Name _____ Date _____

Earth Belongs to You
What You Know

Write answers to these questions.

1. How does Earth get its warmth? _____

2. List different kinds of fuels used in cars and trucks.

   _____

3. Research and give a brief definition of global warming.

   _____

   _____

4. Do you and your family recycle? If so, what items do you recycle?

   _____

   _____

Word Meanings
Definitions

Look for these words as you read your chapter book. When you find one of these words, write its definition.

carbon dioxide: _____

drought: _____

glacier: _____

imagine: _____

mountain: _____

recycle: _____

Earth Belongs to You

	Unfamiliar Words	Word Meanings	Proper Nouns
Chapter 1	bounces covers greenhouse effect ice age neighbors scientist since		Glacier National Park
Chapter 2	arctic ice cap breathe forests global warming levels lose problem silence	carbon dioxide glacier	Amazon River Brazil Haiti Mount Kilimanjaro
Chapter 3	bubbles weather	mountain	Dr. Roger Revelle Hawaii Mauna Loa Pacific Ocean
Chapter 4	floods strong	drought	Africa Hurricane Katrina Lake Chad Louisiana Mississippi River New Orleans
Chapter 5	gasoline oil plastic signed tomorrow	recycle	Kyoto Treaty
Chapter 6	electric electricity	imagine	

Name _____ Date _____

Earth Belongs to You
Chapter 1, "The Greenhouse Effect"

Mark each statement *T* for true or *F* for false.

____ 1. The greenhouse effect is how the sun keeps Earth warm.

____ 2. The top and sides of greenhouses are made of clear glass.

____ 3. Plants and flowers are grown inside greenhouses.

____ 4. There is no way to keep a greenhouse from becoming too warm inside.

____ 5. Air covers Earth.

____ 6. All the light from the sun reaches Earth's surface.

____ 7. Clouds keep Earth from becoming too warm.

____ 8. Light from the sun keeps Earth warm.

____ 9. All the heat from Earth escapes into space.

____ 10. The air around Earth acts like the glass windows of a greenhouse.

Read the question, and write your answer.

Why is it warm inside a greenhouse? _____

_____

_____

Name _____ Date _____

Earth Belongs to You
Chapter 2, "Global Warming"

Fill in the bubble beside the answer for each question.

1. Too much carbon dioxide makes our air
   - Ⓐ brown.
   - Ⓑ thin.
   - Ⓒ thick.

2. Global warming is a problem of
   - Ⓐ thick clouds.
   - Ⓑ too much sunlight.
   - Ⓒ trapped heat.

3. What happens when forests are burned?
   - Ⓐ Carbon dioxide goes into the air.
   - Ⓑ Smoke keeps sunlight from reaching Earth.
   - Ⓒ Oxygen goes into the sky.

4. What is happening at the North Pole?
   - Ⓐ The arctic ice cap is floating away.
   - Ⓑ The arctic ice cap is melting.
   - Ⓒ The arctic ice cap is getting thicker.

Read the question, and write your answer.

Why is too much carbon dioxide in the air a problem?

_____

_____

Name _____ Date _____

Earth Belongs to You
Chapter 3, "Ice Cores"

Mark each statement *T* for true or *F* for false.

____ **1.** Scientists are finding out many things about carbon dioxide.

____ **2.** Scientists are taking ice core samples at the South Pole.

____ **3.** Scientists look at air bubbles in ice cores.

____ **4.** The bubbles are made of carbon dioxide and other gases.

____ **5.** Scientists learn more about air pollution from these bubbles.

____ **6.** A scientist named Dr. Roger Revelle went to the top of Mauna Loa, Alaska's highest mountain.

____ **7.** Dr. Revelle looked for carbon dioxide in the air.

____ **8.** Over the years, Dr. Revelle saw carbon dioxide levels go up.

____ **9.** Lower carbon dioxide levels have been found in the Pacific Ocean.

____ **10.** Too much carbon dioxide is a global warming problem.

Read the question, and write your answer.

Why do you think scientists are interested in learning what Earth's weather was like many years ago?

_____

_____

Name _____ Date _____

Earth Belongs to You
Chapter 4, "Big Weather Problems"

Mark each statement *T* for true or *F* for false.

_____ **1.** Weather problems are part of global warming.

_____ **2.** Floods, droughts, and hurricanes are happening more now than in the past.

_____ **3.** Ocean levels are getting lower.

_____ **4.** Some oceans are getting warmer.

_____ **5.** Warm oceans can mix with cold winds and cause big waves.

_____ **6.** Hurricane Katrina slammed into the shores of Miami, Florida.

_____ **7.** Many people died during Hurricane Katrina.

_____ **8.** The Mississippi River runs through the middle of the United States.

_____ **9.** Lake Chad is the fourth biggest lake in Brazil.

_____ **10.** Over the past few years Lake Chad has grown in size.

Read the question, and write your answer.

What did Lake Chad give the people of Africa?

_____

_____

Name _____ Date _____

Earth Belongs to You
Chapter 5, "It's Not Too Late"

Fill in the bubble beside the answer for each question.

1. Leaders from how many countries got together in 1997 to talk about the global warming problem?

    Ⓐ 15

    Ⓑ 150

    Ⓒ 175

2. The Kyoto Treaty was a deal to

    Ⓐ increase research money to study global warming.

    Ⓑ stop putting so much carbon dioxide in the air.

    Ⓒ keep countries from cutting down forests.

3. What country sends the most carbon dioxide per person into the air?

    Ⓐ the United States

    Ⓑ Great Britain

    Ⓒ Russia

4. Which of the following increases the problem of global warming?

    Ⓐ recycling

    Ⓑ protecting the rain forests

    Ⓒ burning more oil and gas

Read the question, and write your answer.

Who could tell you more about global warming? What could you tell that person about global warming?

_____

_____

Name _____ Date _____

Earth Belongs to You
Chapter 6, "The Right Steps"
Fill in the bubble beside the answer for each question.

1. Running cars on electricity
   - Ⓐ costs more than running cars on gasoline.
   - Ⓑ costs about the same as running cars on gasoline.
   - Ⓒ costs less than running cars on gasoline.

2. Electric cars
   - Ⓐ do not make carbon dioxide.
   - Ⓑ send less carbon dioxide into the air than cars that run on gasoline.
   - Ⓒ would not lower carbon dioxide levels in the air.

3. Today most cars
   - Ⓐ are electric.
   - Ⓑ run on gasoline.
   - Ⓒ run on diesel.

4. What is one change that would occur if all cars ran on electricity?
   - Ⓐ The loud sounds of cars and trucks would be gone.
   - Ⓑ There would be more smoke in the sky.
   - Ⓒ There would be more carbon dioxide in the air.

Read the question, and write your answer.

Describe Earth in 30 years if we fix the global warming problem.

_____

_____

_____

Name _____ Date _____

Earth Belongs to You
Think About It

Write about or give an oral presentation for each question.

1. Use the greenhouse effect to explain global warming.

    _____

    _____

    _____

2. In Haiti, forests are burned to make room for farms. Why do you think people do this?

    _____

    _____

3. Some people don't believe global warming is real. What do you think and why?

    _____

4. What are ways you can help take care of Earth?

    _____

Write About It

Choose one of the questions below. Write your answer on a sheet of paper.

1. Write an ad for an electric car. In your ad, describe why the car is more efficient than a gasoline-powered car and how it will help protect the environment.

2. If you were a scientist, what aspect of global warming would you want to study? Explain your answer.

3. Complete the Content Web for this book.

Earth Belongs to You

Chapter 1 *pages 4 and 5*

*The greenhouse effect is how the sun keeps Earth warm. It gets its	13
name from a real greenhouse. A *greenhouse* is a glass house that helps	26
plants and flowers grow.	30
Clear windows are on the top and sides of a greenhouse. Sunlight	42
comes through the windows. This makes the greenhouse warm inside. If	53
the windows of the greenhouse are opened, heat from the inside escapes.	65
Then the greenhouse won't become too warm.	72
Air covers Earth. The sun sends light to Earth. Much of this light	85
comes through the air. Some* of the light bounces off the air.	97

Chapter 4 *page 19*

*The Mississippi River runs through the middle of the United States.	11
In 1988 a drought happened there. The Mississippi River became very dry.	23
But just five years later, the Mississippi River flooded many shores. The	35
water covered miles and miles of land. Many people lost their homes.	47
In Africa, Lake Chad was once a big body of water. It was the fourth	62
biggest lake in Africa. Lake Chad gave people water for drinking and for	75
their farmland. It also gave them a place to fish. But Lake Chad began to*	90
dry up. Now it has very little water left. In a few years it may be gone.	107

- The target rate for **Anything's Possible** is 90 wcpm. The asterisks (*) mark 90 words.

- Listen to the student read the passage. Count the number of words read in one minute and the number of errors.

- For the reading rate, subtract the number of errors from the total number of words read.

- Have students enter their scores on their **Fluency Graph.** See page 9.

Answer Key

Name _____ Date _____

Earth Belongs to You
What You Know

Write answers to these questions.

1. How does Earth get its warmth? <u>from the sun</u>

2. List different kinds of fuels used in cars and trucks.
   Ideas: gasoline, diesel, ethanol

3. Research and give a brief definition of global warming.
   Global warming refers to an average increase in Earth's temperature.

4. Do you and your family recycle? If so, what items do you recycle?
   Accept reasonable responses.

Word Meanings
Definitions

Look for these words as you read your chapter book. When you find one of these words, write its definition.

carbon dioxide: <u>a gas made up of carbon and oxygen</u>

drought: <u>a long period of dry weather with little or no rain</u>
glacier: <u>a large mass of ice and snow that moves very slowly down</u>
<u>a mountain or across land</u>

imagine: <u>to make up a picture or idea in the mind</u>

mountain: <u>a part of Earth's surface that rises high above the surrounding area</u>

recycle: <u>to put something through a special process so it can be used again</u>

Earth Belongs to You

Name _____ Date _____

Earth Belongs to You
Chapter 1, "The Greenhouse Effect"

Mark each statement *T* for true or *F* for false.

<u>T</u>   1. The greenhouse effect is how the sun keeps Earth warm.

<u>T</u>   2. The top and sides of greenhouses are made of clear glass.

<u>T</u>   3. Plants and flowers are grown inside greenhouses.

<u>F</u>   4. There is no way to keep a greenhouse from becoming too warm inside.

<u>T</u>   5. Air covers Earth.

<u>F</u>   6. All the light from the sun reaches Earth's surface.

<u>F</u>   7. Clouds keep Earth from becoming too warm.

<u>T</u>   8. Light from the sun keeps Earth warm.

<u>F</u>   9. All the heat from Earth escapes into space.

<u>T</u> 10. The air around Earth acts like the glass windows of a greenhouse.

Read the question, and write your answer.

Why is it warm inside a greenhouse? <u>Sunlight comes through the</u>
<u>windows and warms the air; glass keeps the warm air from</u>
<u>escaping.</u>

Earth Belongs to You

Name _____ Date _____

Earth Belongs to You
Chapter 2, "Global Warming"

Fill in the bubble beside the answer for each question.

1. Too much carbon dioxide makes our air
   Ⓐ brown.
   Ⓑ thin.
   ● thick.

2. Global warming is a problem of
   Ⓐ thick clouds.
   Ⓑ too much sunlight.
   ● trapped heat.

3. What happens when forests are burned?
   ● Carbon dioxide goes into the air.
   Ⓑ Smoke keeps sunlight from reaching Earth.
   Ⓒ Oxygen goes into the sky.

4. What is happening at the North Pole?
   Ⓐ The arctic ice cap is floating away.
   ● The arctic ice cap is melting.
   Ⓒ The arctic ice cap is getting thicker.

Read the question, and write your answer.

Why is too much carbon dioxide in the air a problem?
Carbon dioxide makes the air thick. Heat from the sun gets
trapped by the thick air.

Earth Belongs to You

Name _____ Date _____

Earth Belongs to You
Chapter 3, "Ice Cores"

Mark each statement *T* for true or *F* for false.

<u>T</u>   1. Scientists are finding out many things about carbon dioxide.

<u>F</u>   2. Scientists are taking ice core samples at the South Pole.

<u>T</u>   3. Scientists look at air bubbles in ice cores.

<u>T</u>   4. The bubbles are made of carbon dioxide and other gases.

<u>F</u>   5. Scientists learn more about air pollution from these bubbles.

<u>F</u>   6. A scientist named Dr. Roger Revelle went to the top of Mauna Loa, Alaska's highest mountain.

<u>T</u>   7. Dr. Revelle looked for carbon dioxide in the air.

<u>T</u>   8. Over the years, Dr. Revelle saw carbon dioxide levels go up.

<u>F</u>   9. Lower carbon dioxide levels have been found in the Pacific Ocean.

<u>T</u> 10. Too much carbon dioxide is a global warming problem.

Read the question, and write your answer.

Why do you think scientists are interested in learning what Earth's weather was like many years ago?
to compare Earth's current weather to past weather; to look for
changes in weather patterns

Earth Belongs to You

Answer Key

Name _____ Date _____

Earth Belongs to You
Chapter 4, "Big Weather Problems"
Mark each statement *T* for true or *F* for false.

__T__ 1. Weather problems are part of global warming.

__T__ 2. Floods, droughts, and hurricanes are happening more now than in the past.

__F__ 3. Ocean levels are getting lower.

__T__ 4. Some oceans are getting warmer.

__T__ 5. Warm oceans can mix with cold winds and cause big waves.

__F__ 6. Hurricane Katrina slammed into the shores of Miami, Florida.

__T__ 7. Many people died during Hurricane Katrina.

__T__ 8. The Mississippi River runs through the middle of the United States.

__F__ 9. Lake Chad is the fourth biggest lake in Brazil.

__F__ 10. Over the past few years Lake Chad has grown in size.

Read the question, and write your answer.

What did Lake Chad give the people of Africa?

water for drinking and for their farmland; a place to fish

Anything's Possible • Book 6   77

Earth Belongs to You

Name _____ Date _____

Earth Belongs to You
Chapter 5, "It's Not Too Late"
Fill in the bubble beside the answer for each question.

1. Leaders from how many countries got together in 1997 to talk about the global warming problem?
   Ⓐ 15
   ● 150
   Ⓒ 175

2. The Kyoto Treaty was a deal to
   Ⓐ increase research money to study global warming.
   ● stop putting so much carbon dioxide in the air.
   Ⓒ keep countries from cutting down forests.

3. What country sends the most carbon dioxide per person into the air?
   ● the United States
   Ⓑ Great Britain
   Ⓒ Russia

4. Which of the following increases the problem of global warming?
   Ⓐ recycling
   Ⓑ protecting the rain forests
   ● burning more oil and gas

Read the question, and write your answer.

Who could tell you more about global warming? What could you tell that person about global warming?

an environmental scientist; accept reasonable responses

78   Anything's Possible • Book 6

Earth Belongs to You

Name _____ Date _____

Earth Belongs to You
Chapter 6, "The Right Steps"
Fill in the bubble beside the answer for each question.

1. Running cars on electricity
   Ⓐ costs more than running cars on gasoline.
   Ⓑ costs about the same as running cars on gasoline.
   ● costs less than running cars on gasoline.

2. Electric cars
   ● do not make carbon dioxide.
   Ⓑ send less carbon dioxide into the air than cars that run on gasoline.
   Ⓒ would not lower carbon dioxide levels in the air.

3. Today most cars
   Ⓐ are electric.
   ● run on gasoline.
   Ⓒ run on diesel.

4. What is one change that would occur if all cars ran on electricity?
   ● The loud sounds of cars and trucks would be gone.
   Ⓑ There would be more smoke in the sky.
   Ⓒ There would be more carbon dioxide in the air.

Read the question, and write your answer.

Describe Earth in 30 years if we fix the global warming problem.

lower carbon dioxide levels; rain forests have grown back;

cleaner air

Anything's Possible • Book 6   79

Earth Belongs to You

Name _____ Date _____

Earth Belongs to You
Think About It
Write about or give an oral presentation for each question.

1. Use the greenhouse effect to explain global warming.
   The air around Earth acts like the glass windows of a greenhouse.
   Sunlight comes through the air and warms Earth. Air mostly made of
   carbon dioxide is like windows of a greenhouse that are stuck shut.

2. In Haiti, forests are burned to make room for farms. Why do you think people do this?
   poverty; need to grow food; lack of knowledge about global
   warming

3. Some people don't believe global warming is real. What do you think and why?
   Accept reasonable responses.

4. What are ways you can help take care of Earth?
   Accept reasonable responses.

Write About It
Choose one of the questions below. Write your answer on a sheet of paper.

1. Write an ad for an electric car. In your ad, describe why the car is more efficient than a gasoline-powered car and how it will help protect the environment.

2. If you were a scientist, what aspect of global warming would you want to study? Explain your answer.

3. Complete the Content Web for this book.

80   Anything's Possible • Book 6

Earth Belongs to You

Name _____ Date _____

Treasure Island
What You Know

Write answers to these questions.

1. What is a pirate? What do they do? How do they live?

   _____

2. What do you think it would be like to discover a hidden treasure?

   _____

3. Not all treasure is gold or money. What other kinds of treasures are there?

   _____

4. What would you do if you knew that your friends were lying to you?
   Would you let them know right away? Explain your answer.

   _____

Word Meanings
Synonyms and Antonyms

Look for these words as you read your chapter book. When you find a word, write a synonym or antonym for the word.

Synonyms

cook: _____

swamp: _____

shore: _____

Antonyms

death: _____

skinny: _____

true: _____

Treasure Island

Unfamiliar Words	Word Meanings	Proper Nouns	
captain change died inn pirate treasure visit	death	Captain Flint Dr. Livesey Jim Hawkins Squire Trelawney Treasure Island	**Chapter 1**
ar matey parrot	cook	Captain Smollet *Hispaniola* Long John Silver	**Chapter 2**
anchor thought	shore skinny	Ben Gunn England	**Chapter 3**
fight stockade	swamp		**Chapter 4**
climbing dagger			**Chapter 5**
empty	true		**Chapter 6**

Name _____ Date _____

Treasure Island
Chapter 1, "The Old Captain"

Fill in the bubble beside the answer for each question.

1. Who is Jim?
   - Ⓐ a pirate's son
   - Ⓑ a doctor's son
   - Ⓒ a boy who works at a family-owned inn

2. Who does the captain tell Jim to watch out for?
   - Ⓐ pirates who might break into the inn
   - Ⓑ a man with one leg
   - Ⓒ a pirate named Black Dog

3. What does Jim find inside the sea chest?
   - Ⓐ silver coins
   - Ⓑ a paper with the mark of death
   - Ⓒ a map and some gold

4. Who allows Jim to look for the treasure?
   - Ⓐ Squire Trelawney
   - Ⓑ Jim's father
   - Ⓒ Jim's mother

Read the question, and write your answer.

Why do you think Dr. Livesey and Squire Trelawney are so willing to help Jim search for the treasure?

_____

_____

Name _____ Date _____

Treasure Island
Chapter 2, "Long John Silver"

Mark each statement *T* for true or *F* for false.

_____ **1.** Silver was the cook on the *Hispaniola*.

_____ **2.** Silver's leg was made of metal.

_____ **3.** Silver had a talking parrot.

_____ **4.** Captain Smollett thought the sailors Squire Trelawney had picked were good sailors.

_____ **5.** Jim was looking for an apple when he fell into the box.

_____ **6.** Silver knew Jim was listening to him when he was talking about the treasure map.

_____ **7.** Silver wants the gold that Jim brought aboard the ship.

_____ **8.** Silver is a pirate.

_____ **9.** There aren't any pirates on the ship.

_____ **10.** Squire Trelawney decides not to tell Captain Smollett about the pirates on the ship.

Read the question, and write your answer.

Why do you think Squire Trelawney did not listen to Captain Smollett and take his advice?

_____

_____

Name _____ Date _____

Treasure Island
Chapter 3, "Going Ashore"

Number the events in order from 1 to 5.

_____ Silver's pirates board two boats and set out for shore.

_____ Ben Gunn tells Jim about himself.

_____ Night falls, and Jim can see their flag on the *Hispaniola's* mast.

_____ Silver and his pirates reach shore.

_____ Jim meets Gunn.

Mark each statement *T* for true or *F* for false.

_____ **1.** Jim gets to the island before Silver and his men.

_____ **2.** Silver sees Jim on the island and grabs him.

_____ **3.** Gunn had sailed to the island with Captain Flint.

_____ **4.** Gunn has been living on the island for three years.

_____ **5.** Flint did not hide his treasure very well.

Read the question, and write your answer.

How is Gunn described?

_____

_____

Name _____ Date _____

Treasure Island
Chapter 4, "The Stockade"

Number the events in order from 1 to 5.

_____ Jim tells Dr. Livesey about Gunn.

_____ Dr. Livesey meets Jim at the stockade.

_____ The pirates fire at Dr. Livesey's boat and sink it.

_____ Dr. Livesey leaves the ship to look for Jim.

_____ Dr. Livesey tells Jim some pirates are hiding in a swamp.

Number the events in order from 6 to 10.

_____ Dr. Livesey tells Jim the pirates might get sick in a few days.

_____ The pirates begin to fire again.

_____ Silver sees Dr. Livesey, Jim, and the rest of their men.

_____ Silver tells Dr. Livesey that he will get him back to England if Dr. Livesey gives him the map.

_____ Jim and the others run back into the stockade.

Read the question, and write your answer.

What do you think will happen in the next chapter?

_____

_____

_____

Name _____ Date _____

Treasure Island
Chapter 5, "Jim and the Pirate"

Fill in the bubble beside the answer for each question.

1. What does Jim notice about the *Hispaniola?*

    Ⓐ The pirate flag is up.

    Ⓑ The ship is missing.

    Ⓒ The ship is drifting away from the island.

2. Why does Jim take Gunn's boat to the *Hispaniola?*

    Ⓐ to get more supplies

    Ⓑ to try to capture the ship from the pirates

    Ⓒ to cut the ship's anchor rope

3. How does Jim escape from the pirate who is chasing him?

    Ⓐ He shakes the ropes so hard the pirate falls.

    Ⓑ He gets back into Gunn's boat.

    Ⓒ He jumps into the water and swims back to shore.

4. Where does Jim run into Silver?

    Ⓐ on the *Hispaniola*

    Ⓑ in the stockade

    Ⓒ on Gunn's boat

Read the question, and write your answer.

Compare and contrast the actions of Jim and his men with those of Silver and the other pirates.

_____

_____

_____

Name _____ Date _____

Treasure Island
Chapter 6, "X Marks the Spot"

Mark each statement *T* for true or *F* for false.

_____ **1.** Dr. Livesey gives Silver the treasure map, so Silver lets him go.

_____ **2.** None of the pirates are ill.

_____ **3.** Silver wants to hurt Jim and the rest of the good men.

_____ **4.** Silver wins back his men when he shows them he has the treasure map.

_____ **5.** Silver orders his men to keep Jim safe.

_____ **6.** While the pirates are searching for the treasure they find the bones of a man.

_____ **7.** The bones the pirates find are the bones of Gunn.

_____ **8.** Instead of treasure, the pirates find an empty hole in the ground.

_____ **9.** Dr. Livesey does not know that Gunn put the treasure in a cave.

_____ **10.** Dr. Livesey says he wants to go treasure hunting again.

Read the question, and write your answer.

Why do you think Dr. Livesey and the others give Silver money and a boat?

_____

_____

_____

Name _____ Date _____

Treasure Island
Think About It

Think about or give an oral presentation for each question.

1. What changes Jim's mind about Silver at the end of the story?

   _____

2. Why do you think Jim traveled with Squire Trelawney despite knowing that pirates were after the treasure and that it could be very dangerous? Explain. _____

   _____

3. Jim accidentally overheard Silver talking about the map. How do you think the story would have ended if Jim had not known that Silver and several other sailors were pirates?

   _____

4. Do you think Silver remained a pirate after he left the island? Why or why not?

   _____

Write About It

Choose one of the questions below. Write your answer on a sheet of paper.

1. Pretend you are Jim. Write a journal entry on the day you returned to England. Describe your adventure and include how it felt to be in so many dangerous situations, how you met Gunn, and how your feelings about Silver have changed.

2. Research well-known pirates. Pick one and write a newspaper article detailing that pirate's life.

3. Complete the Story Grammar Map for this book.

Treasure Island

Chapter 1 *page 5*

*"Jim," he said, "take care of my sea chest. Others will come after it!"	14
Those were his last words.	19

Soon after the captain died, my father died too. I was afraid other	32
pirates would come. Mother and I went to the captain's room. We opened	45
the sea chest. Inside we found a map, some gold, and a few other things. I	61
put the map inside my shirt. Then we went outside and hid.	73

The captain was right. More pirates broke into the inn. They wanted the	86
map! If they found* it on me, what would they do?	97

Chapter 3 *page 13*

*Silver seemed to be looking right at me. Then he smiled. I thought he	14
had seen me. But he turned and walked the other way. His men followed	28
him.	29

I bolted deep into the trees, breathing hard. Suddenly a skinny hand	41
grabbed me. Before I could scream the hand covered my mouth. I turned	54
around and saw the oddest-looking man I had ever seen.	64

The man said his name was Ben Gunn. He looked more like an animal than	79
a man. His skin was deeply tanned. His ears stuck out.* And his long hair	94
flowed down his back.	98

- The target rate for **Anything's Possible** is 90 wcpm. The asterisks (*) mark 90 words.

- Listen to the student read the passage. Count the number of words read in one minute and the number of errors.

- For the reading rate, subtract the number of errors from the total number of words read.

- Have students enter their scores on their **Fluency Graph.** See page 9.

Answer Key

Building Background

Name _____ Date _____

Treasure Island
What You Know
Write answers to these questions.

1. What is a pirate? What do they do? How do they live?
   a person who attacks and robs ships; accept reasonable responses

2. What do you think it would be like to discover a hidden treasure?
   Ideas: exciting, fun, scary

3. Not all treasure is gold or money. What other kinds of treasures are there?
   Ideas: friends, family

4. What would you do if you knew that your friends were lying to you? Would you let them know right away? Explain your answer.
   Accept reasonable responses.

Word Meanings
Synonyms and Antonyms
Look for these words as you read your chapter book. When you find a word, write a synonym or antonym for the word.

Synonyms
cook: **chef, food preparer**
swamp: **bog, marsh**
shore: **beach, coast**

Antonyms
death: **birth, life**
skinny: **fat, overweight**
true: **false, untrue**

Anything's Possible • Book 7

Treasure Island

Chapter Quiz

Name _____ Date _____

Treasure Island
Chapter 1, "The Old Captain"
Fill in the bubble beside the answer for each question.

1. Who is Jim?
   - Ⓐ a pirate's son
   - Ⓑ a doctor's son
   - ● a boy who works at a family-owned inn

2. Who does the captain tell Jim to watch out for?
   - Ⓐ pirates who might break into the inn
   - ● a man with one leg
   - Ⓒ a pirate named Black Dog

3. What does Jim find inside the sea chest?
   - Ⓐ silver coins
   - Ⓑ a paper with the mark of death
   - ● a map and some gold

4. Who allows Jim to look for the treasure?
   - Ⓐ Squire Trelawney
   - Ⓑ Jim's father
   - ● Jim's mother

Read the question, and write your answer.

Why do you think Dr. Livesey and Squire Trelawney are so willing to help Jim search for the treasure?
Ideas: They want to make sure Jim and his mother are safe; they
are greedy men who want to find the treasure for themselves.

Anything's Possible • Book 7

Treasure Island

Chapter Quiz

Name _____ Date _____

Treasure Island
Chapter 2, "Long John Silver"
Mark each statement *T* for true or *F* for false.

T 1. Silver was the cook on the *Hispaniola*.
F 2. Silver's leg was made of metal.
T 3. Silver had a talking parrot.
F 4. Captain Smollett thought the sailors Squire Trelawney had picked were good sailors.
T 5. Jim was looking for an apple when he fell into the box.
F 6. Silver knew Jim was listening to him when he was talking about the treasure map.
F 7. Silver wants the gold that Jim brought aboard the ship.
T 8. Silver is a pirate.
F 9. There aren't any pirates on the ship.
F 10. Squire Trelawney decides not to tell Captain Smollett about the pirates on the ship.

Read the question, and write your answer.

Why do you think Squire Trelawney did not listen to Captain Smollett and take his advice?
Idea: Trelawney thought he knew better.

Anything's Possible • Book 7

Treasure Island

Chapter Quiz

Name _____ Date _____

Treasure Island
Chapter 3, "Going Ashore"
Number the events in order from 1 to 5.

1 Silver's pirates board two boats and set out for shore.
4 Ben Gunn tells Jim about himself.
5 Night falls, and Jim can see their flag on the *Hispaniola's* mast.
2 Silver and his pirates reach shore.
3 Jim meets Gunn.

Mark each statement *T* for true or *F* for false.

T 1. Jim gets to the island before Silver and his men.
F 2. Silver sees Jim on the island and grabs him.
T 3. Gunn had sailed to the island with Captain Flint.
T 4. Gunn has been living on the island for three years.
F 5. Flint did not hide his treasure very well.

Read the question, and write your answer.

How is Gunn described?
looked more like animal than man; skin was tan; ears
stuck out; long hair flowed down his back

Anything's Possible • Book 7

Treasure Island

Anything's Possible • Book 7

Name _____ Date _____

Treasure Island
Chapter 4, "The Stockade"
Number the events in order from 1 to 5.

_4_ Jim tells Dr. Livesey about Gunn.

_3_ Dr. Livesey meets Jim at the stockade.

_2_ The pirates fire at Dr. Livesey's boat and sink it.

_1_ Dr. Livesey leaves the ship to look for Jim.

_5_ Dr. Livesey tells Jim some pirates are hiding in a swamp.

Number the events in order from 6 to 10.

_6_ Dr. Livesey tells Jim the pirates might get sick in a few days.

_9_ The pirates begin to fire again.

_7_ Silver sees Dr. Livesey, Jim, and the rest of their men.

_8_ Silver tells Dr. Livesey that he will get him back to England if Dr. Livesey gives him the map.

_10_ Jim and the others run back into the stockade.

Read the question, and write your answer.

What do you think will happen in the next chapter?
Accept reasonable responses.

_____

_____

Anything's Possible • Book 7   89

Treasure Island

Name _____ Date _____

Treasure Island
Chapter 5, "Jim and the Pirate"
Fill in the bubble beside the answer for each question.

1. What does Jim notice about the *Hispaniola?*
   ● The pirate flag is up.
   Ⓑ The ship is missing.
   Ⓒ The ship is drifting away from the island.

2. Why does Jim take Gunn's boat to the *Hispaniola?*
   Ⓐ to get more supplies
   Ⓑ to try to capture the ship from the pirates
   ● to cut the ship's anchor rope

3. How does Jim escape from the pirate who is chasing him?
   ● He shakes the ropes so hard the pirate falls.
   Ⓑ He gets back into Gunn's boat.
   Ⓒ He jumps into the water and swims back to shore.

4. Where does Jim run into Silver?
   Ⓐ on the *Hispaniola*
   ● in the stockade
   Ⓒ on Gunn's boat

Read the question, and write your answer.

Compare and contrast the actions of Jim and his men with those of Silver and the other pirates.
Jim and his men are the "good guys"; the doctor is helping the
sick pirates; Silver and the pirates are the "bad guys"; they are
willing to do anything in order to get the treasure.

90   Anything's Possible • Book 7

Treasure Island

Name _____ Date _____

Treasure Island
Chapter 6, "X Marks the Spot"
Mark each statement *T* for true or *F* for false.

_T_ 1. Dr. Livesey gives Silver the treasure map, so Silver lets him go.

_F_ 2. None of the pirates are ill.

_F_ 3. Silver wants to hurt Jim and the rest of the good men.

_T_ 4. Silver wins back his men when he shows them he has the treasure map.

_T_ 5. Silver orders his men to keep Jim safe.

_T_ 6. While the pirates are searching for the treasure they find the bones of a man.

_F_ 7. The bones the pirates find are the bones of Gunn.

_T_ 8. Instead of treasure, the pirates find an empty hole in the ground.

_F_ 9. Dr. Livesey does not know that Gunn put the treasure in a cave.

_F_ 10. Dr. Livesey says he wants to go treasure hunting again.

Read the question, and write your answer.

Why do you think Dr. Livesey and the others give Silver money and a boat?
Ideas: They do not think he is completely bad; he agreed to help
protect them and take them back to England.

_____

Anything's Possible • Book 7   91

Treasure Island

Name _____ Date _____

Treasure Island
Think About It

Think about or give an oral presentation for each question.

1. What changes Jim's mind about Silver at the end of the story?
   Silver keeps Jim and his friends safe from the pirates and helps them get to their ship safely.

2. Why do you think Jim traveled with Squire Trelawney despite knowing that pirates were after the treasure and that it could be very dangerous? Explain. **Ideas: needed money; liked the idea of the adventure; didn't realize the extent of the danger**

3. Jim accidentally overheard Silver talking about the map. How do you think the story would have ended if Jim had not known that Silver and several other sailors were pirates?
   Accept reasonable responses.

4. Do you think Silver remained a pirate after he left the island? Why or why not?
   Accept reasonable responses.

Write About It

Choose one of the questions below. Write your answer on a sheet of paper.

1. Pretend you are Jim. Write a journal entry on the day you returned to England. Describe your adventure and include how it felt to be in so many dangerous situations, how you met Gunn, and how your feelings about Silver have changed.

2. Research well-known pirates. Pick one and write a newspaper article detailing that pirate's life.

3. Complete the Story Grammar Map for this book.

92   Anything's Possible • Book 7

Treasure Island

Name _____ Date _____

Gulliver's Travels
What You Know

Write answers to these questions.

1. What is a satire? _____

2. What do you think it would be like to live in a place where you are completely different from everyone else?

   _____

   _____

3. How would you communicate with people if they did not understand your language and you did not understand their language?

   _____

4. What kinds of things can you do to help newcomers feel welcome at your school or in your community?

   _____

Word Meanings
Matching

Look for these words as you read your chapter book. When you find a word, draw a line to connect the word with the correct definition.

thumb   a slender stick that is shot from a bow

language   a field in which wheat is grown

thimble   a strong bird of prey that has sharp eyesight

arrow   the speech of a certain nation, group, or people

wheat field   a small metal or plastic cap used in sewing

eagle   the short, thick finger nearest the wrist

Gulliver's Travels

Unfamiliar Words	Word Meanings	Proper Nouns	
built quiet soldiers	arrow	*Antelope* England Gulliver Lilliput	Chapter 1
brought giant pointed	thumb		Chapter 2
gathered emperor face peace tied	language	Blefuscu Blefuscan	Chapter 3
blew	wheat field	*Adventure* Brobdingnag	Chapter 4
friend placed sword taught welcome	thimble	Glumdalclitch	Chapter 5
capital court piece	eagle		Chapter 6

Name _____ Date _____

Gulliver's Travels
Chapter 1, "A Big Man in Lilliput"

Mark each statement *T* for true or *F* for false.

_____ 1. Gulliver is a doctor from France.

_____ 2. Gulliver's ship is wrecked during a storm.

_____ 3. When Gulliver awakes, he is tied to the ground.

_____ 4. Gulliver breaks free of the ropes holding him down.

_____ 5. The Lilliputians are bigger and taller than Gulliver.

_____ 6. The Lilliputians attack Gulliver with bows and arrows.

_____ 7. Gulliver decides to fight back to try to save his life.

_____ 8. Gulliver is seriously wounded by the Lilliputians.

_____ 9. The Lilliputians speak the same language as Gulliver.

_____ 10. The Lilliputians build a new ship for Gulliver.

Read the question, and write your answer.

What do you think the well-dressed man might be saying to Gulliver?

_____

_____

_____

Name _____ Date _____

Gulliver's Travels
Chapter 2, "Life in Lilliput"

Fill in the bubble beside the answer for each question.

1. Why does Gulliver point to his mouth?
   Ⓐ He intends to eat the Lilliputians.
   Ⓑ He is hungry and wants food.
   Ⓒ He wants water to drink.

2. Gulliver's new home looks like a
   Ⓐ doll's house.
   Ⓑ log cabin.
   Ⓒ big house.

3. When some men shot arrows at Gulliver, soldiers
   Ⓐ brought some of the men to Gulliver.
   Ⓑ surrounded Gulliver in order to protect him.
   Ⓒ joined in the attack.

4. People no longer feared Gulliver because they
   Ⓐ knew he would protect them.
   Ⓑ knew that their own soldiers would protect them.
   Ⓒ knew he would not kill them.

Read the question, and write your answer.

How is Gulliver able to make friends with the Lilliputians?

_____

_____

Name _____ Date _____

Gulliver's Travels
Chapter 3, "Trouble with Blefuscu"

Number the events in order from 1 to 5.

____ The emperor says Blefuscu plans to invade Lilliput.

____ Gulliver learns the Lilliputian language.

____ Gulliver gathers hooks and ties each hook to a rope.

____ Gulliver goes to see the Blefuscan fleet.

____ The emperor of Lilliput and Gulliver visit with each other.

Number the events in order from 6 to 10.

____ The Blefuscans help Gulliver fix his ship.

____ Gulliver becomes a hero in Lilliput.

____ Lilliput and Blefuscu make peace.

____ Gulliver returns to England.

____ Gulliver hooks the Blefuscan ships and pulls them out to sea.

Read the question, and write your answer.

Why do you think the Blefuscans decide to make peace with Lilliput?

_____

_____

Name _____ Date _____

Gulliver's Travels
Chapter 4, "Brobdingnag"

Mark each statement *T* for true or *F* for false.

_____ **1.** After his last adventure, Gulliver does not want to leave England again.

_____ **2.** Gulliver's ship becomes lost at sea.

_____ **3.** The shipwrecked sailors go to look for drinking water.

_____ **4.** Gulliver and the sailors explore the land together.

_____ **5.** Gulliver finds giants.

Number the events in order from 1 to 5.

_____ Gulliver tries to hide.

_____ A giant shouts to his friends with cutting hooks.

_____ A giant takes Gulliver to the owner of the farm.

_____ Gulliver runs through a wheat field.

_____ Gulliver screams when he sees that a giant is going to step on him.

Read the question, and write your answer.

How does Gulliver's new situation differ from his last adventure?

_____

_____

Name _____ Date _____

Gulliver's Travels
Chapter 5, "Life on the Farm"

Fill in the bubble beside the answer for each question.

1. What does the farmer do with Gulliver?
   - Ⓐ He puts Gulliver to work cutting wheat.
   - Ⓑ He gives Gulliver to his son as a servant.
   - Ⓒ He takes Gulliver home and protects him.

2. Where does Gulliver sleep?
   - Ⓐ in a doll's bed
   - Ⓑ on the lunch table
   - Ⓒ in a regular bed

3. Glumdalclitch teaches Gulliver how to
   - Ⓐ play with dolls.
   - Ⓑ speak her language.
   - Ⓒ make friends with the giants.

4. The farmer puts Gulliver to work
   - Ⓐ performing.
   - Ⓑ harvesting.
   - Ⓒ teaching.

Read the question, and write your answer.

Do you think Gulliver will be able to escape from Brobdingnag? Explain your answer.

_____

_____

Name _____ Date _____

Gulliver's Travels
Chapter 6, "Going Home"

Mark each statement *T* for true or *F* for false.

_____ **1.** Gulliver performs one show per day.

_____ **2.** Gulliver has a lot of time to rest.

_____ **3.** The farmer sells Gulliver to the queen.

_____ **4.** The farmer is sad to lose Gulliver.

_____ **5.** The queen hires Glumdalclitch to stay at the court.

_____ **6.** At the court, Gulliver lives in a wooden box.

_____ **7.** Gulliver feels very safe at the court.

_____ **8.** One day Gulliver is knocked over when an apple hits him in the back.

_____ **9.** An eagle picks up Gulliver's box.

_____ **10.** The eagle takes Gulliver back to England.

Read the question, and write your answer.

What did Gulliver learn from his time in Brobdingnag?

_____

_____

Name _____ Date _____

Gulliver's Travels
Think About It

Write about or give an oral presentation for each question.

1. Gulliver spends a lot of time away from home. Why do you think people like to travel and explore new places? Explain your answer.

   _____

2. How do you think it would feel to be a giant compared to everyone around you?

   _____

3. During his travels, Gulliver learns two new languages. What does this tell us about Gulliver?

   _____

4. What are some of the lessons Gulliver learns during his adventures?

   _____

Write About It

Choose one of the questions below. Write your answer on a sheet of paper.

1. Imagine that you are Gulliver. Write a letter from Lilliput or Brobdingnag to your family. Use sensory details like taste, touch, smell, sight, and sound to describe your experiences.

2. If you had the opportunity to travel around the world, what countries would you visit? Describe the countries and what you would expect to see.

3. Find another story from *Gulliver's Travels,* and read it. Write a summary of the story.

4. Complete the Compare and Contrast Chart for this book.

Gulliver's Travels

Chapter 2 *page 6*

*After I ate I fell asleep. While I slept, the tiny people moved me to	15
the town. Later they told me the town was named Lilliput.	26

When I woke up I was in front of a big house. There was no one in it.	44
This was to be my new home. It looked like a big doll's house. The door	60
only came up to my chest. I had to get down on the ground to get inside.	77

The people were afraid of me. They were so tiny that I must* have	91
seemed like a giant to them.	97

Chapter 4 *page 15*

*A few months after I got home from Lilliput I went to sea again. My	15
new ship was called the *Adventure*. Six months after we left England a	28
storm blew us far off track. We were lost.	37

After many weeks of floating we found land. The sailors went one	49
way to look for water to drink. I walked the other way. When I saw the	65
sailors go back to the ship I started to go back too. Then I saw something	81
that stopped me. A giant followed them into the* sea. It looked like a man.	96
But it was ten times taller than a man.	105

- The target rate for **Anything's Possible** is 90 wcpm. The asterisks (*) mark 90 words.
- Listen to the student read the passage. Count the number of words read in one minute and the number of errors.
- For the reading rate, subtract the number of errors from the total number of words read.
- Have students enter their scores on their **Fluency Graph.** See page 9.

Answer Key

Building Background

Name _____ Date _____

Gulliver's Travels
What You Know
Write answers to these questions.

1. What is a satire? <u>a story that makes fun of people, ideas, habits, or customs</u>

2. What do you think it would be like to live in a place where you are completely different from everyone else?
   Answers will vary.

3. How would you communicate with people if they did not understand your language and you did not understand their language?
   Ideas: hand signals, pointing, drawing pictures

4. What kinds of things can you do to help newcomers feel welcome at your school or in your community?
   Accept reasonable responses.

Word Meanings
Matching
Look for these words as you read your chapter book. When you find a word, draw a line to connect the word with the correct definition.

thumb — the short, thick finger nearest the wrist
language — the speech of a certain nation, group, or people
thimble — a small metal or plastic cap used in sewing
arrow — a slender stick that is shot from a bow
wheat field — a field in which wheat is grown
eagle — a strong bird of prey that has sharp eyesight

96   Anything's Possible • Book 8

Gulliver's Travels

Chapter Quiz

Name _____ Date _____

Gulliver's Travels
Chapter 1, "A Big Man in Lilliput"
Mark each statement *T* for true or *F* for false.

<u>F</u> 1. Gulliver is a doctor from France.
<u>T</u> 2. Gulliver's ship is wrecked during a storm.
<u>T</u> 3. When Gulliver awakes, he is tied to the ground.
<u>T</u> 4. Gulliver breaks free of the ropes holding him down.
<u>F</u> 5. The Lilliputians are bigger and taller than Gulliver.
<u>T</u> 6. The Lilliputians attack Gulliver with bows and arrows.
<u>F</u> 7. Gulliver decides to fight back to try to save his life.
<u>F</u> 8. Gulliver is seriously wounded by the Lilliputians.
<u>F</u> 9. The Lilliputians speak the same language as Gulliver.
<u>F</u> 10. The Lilliputians build a new ship for Gulliver.

Read the question, and write your answer.

What do you think the well-dressed man might be saying to Gulliver?
Ideas: asking about his identity and his intentions; telling
Gulliver about the Lilliputians

98   Anything's Possible • Book 8

Gulliver's Travels

Chapter Quiz

Name _____ Date _____

Gulliver's Travels
Chapter 2, "Life in Lilliput"
Fill in the bubble beside the answer for each question.

1. Why does Gulliver point to his mouth?
   Ⓐ He intends to eat the Lilliputians.
   ● He is hungry and wants food.
   Ⓒ He wants water to drink.

2. Gulliver's new home looks like a
   ● doll's house.
   Ⓑ log cabin.
   Ⓒ big house.

3. When some men shot arrows at Gulliver, soldiers
   ● brought some of the men to Gulliver.
   Ⓑ surrounded Gulliver in order to protect him.
   Ⓒ joined in the attack.

4. People no longer feared Gulliver because they
   Ⓐ knew he would protect them.
   Ⓑ knew that their own soldiers would protect them.
   ● knew he would not kill them.

Read the question, and write your answer.

How is Gulliver able to make friends with the Lilliputians?
He shows that he will not hurt them by holding a man near his
mouth and then putting the man down.

Anything's Possible • Book 8   99

Gulliver's Travels

Chapter Quiz

Name _____ Date _____

Gulliver's Travels
Chapter 3, "Trouble with Blefuscu"
Number the events in order from 1 to 5.

<u>3</u> The emperor says Blefuscu plans to invade Lilliput.
<u>1</u> Gulliver learns the Lilliputian language.
<u>4</u> Gulliver gathers hooks and ties each hook to a rope.
<u>5</u> Gulliver goes to see the Blefuscan fleet.
<u>2</u> The emperor of Lilliput and Gulliver visit with each other.

Number the events in order from 6 to 10.

<u>9</u> The Blefuscans help Gulliver fix his ship.
<u>7</u> Gulliver becomes a hero in Lilliput.
<u>8</u> Lilliput and Blefuscu make peace.
<u>10</u> Gulliver returns to England.
<u>6</u> Gulliver hooks the Blefuscan ships and pulls them out to sea.

Read the question, and write your answer.

Why do you think the Blefuscans decide to make peace with Lilliput?
They saw that with Gulliver helping the Lilliputians, they could
not win a war against them.

100   Anything's Possible • Book 8

Gulliver's Travels

Chapter Quiz

Name _____ Date _____

Gulliver's Travels
Chapter 4, "Brobdingnag"

Mark each statement *T* for true or *F* for false.

_F_ 1. After his last adventure, Gulliver does not want to leave England again.

_T_ 2. Gulliver's ship becomes lost at sea.

_T_ 3. The shipwrecked sailors go to look for drinking water.

_F_ 4. Gulliver and the sailors explore the land together.

_T_ 5. Gulliver finds giants.

Number the events in order from 1 to 5.

_2_ Gulliver tries to hide.

_3_ A giant shouts to his friends with cutting hooks.

_5_ A giant takes Gulliver to the owner of the farm.

_1_ Gulliver runs through a wheat field.

_4_ Gulliver screams when he sees that a giant is going to step on him.

Read the question, and write your answer.

How does Gulliver's new situation differ from his last adventure?

In Lilliput, Gulliver was a giant; in Brobdingnag, Gulliver is

dwarfed by giants.

Anything's Possible • Book 8   101

Gulliver's Travels

Chapter Quiz

Name _____ Date _____

Gulliver's Travels
Chapter 5, "Life on the Farm"

Fill in the bubble beside the answer for each question.

1. What does the farmer do with Gulliver?
   - Ⓐ He puts Gulliver to work cutting wheat.
   - Ⓑ He gives Gulliver to his son as a servant.
   - ● He takes Gulliver home and protects him.

2. Where does Gulliver sleep?
   - ● in a doll's bed
   - Ⓑ on the lunch table
   - Ⓒ in a regular bed

3. Glumdalclitch teaches Gulliver how to
   - Ⓐ play with dolls.
   - ● speak her language.
   - Ⓒ make friends with the giants.

4. The farmer puts Gulliver to work
   - ● performing.
   - Ⓑ harvesting.
   - Ⓒ teaching.

Read the question, and write your answer.

Do you think Gulliver will be able to escape from Brobdingnag? Explain your answer.

Accept reasonable responses.

102   Anything's Possible • Book 8

Gulliver's Travels

Chapter Quiz

Name _____ Date _____

Gulliver's Travels
Chapter 6, "Going Home"

Mark each statement *T* for true or *F* for false.

_F_ 1. Gulliver performs one show per day.

_F_ 2. Gulliver has a lot of time to rest.

_T_ 3. The farmer sells Gulliver to the queen.

_F_ 4. The farmer is sad to lose Gulliver.

_T_ 5. The queen hires Glumdalclitch to stay at the court.

_T_ 6. At the court, Gulliver lives in a wooden box.

_F_ 7. Gulliver feels very safe at the court.

_T_ 8. One day Gulliver is knocked over when an apple hits him in the back.

_T_ 9. An eagle picks up Gulliver's box.

_F_ 10. The eagle takes Gulliver back to England.

Read the question, and write your answer.

What did Gulliver learn from his time in Brobdingnag?

Accept reasonable responses.

Anything's Possible • Book 8   103

Gulliver's Travels

Thinking and Writing

Name _____ Date _____

Gulliver's Travels
Think About It

Write about or give an oral presentation for each question.

1. Gulliver spends a lot of time away from home. Why do you think people like to travel and explore new places? Explain your answer.
   Accept reasonable responses.

2. How do you think it would feel to be a giant compared to everyone around you?
   Accept reasonable responses.

3. During his travels, Gulliver learns two new languages. What does this tell us about Gulliver?
   curious; wants to learn; understands the importance of communication

4. What are some of the lessons Gulliver learns during his adventures?
   Accept reasonable responses.

Write About It

Choose one of the questions below. Write your answer on a sheet of paper.

1. Imagine that you are Gulliver. Write a letter from Lilliput or Brobdingnag to your family. Use sensory details like taste, touch, smell, sight, and sound to describe your experiences.

2. If you had the opportunity to travel around the world, what countries would you visit? Describe the countries and what you would expect to see.

3. Find another story from *Gulliver's Travels,* and read it. Write a summary of the story.

4. Complete the Compare and Contrast Chart for this book.

104   Anything's Possible • Book 8

Gulliver's Travels

Name _____ Date _____

Adventures on the Nile
Book Report Form

List the key points from the book you read.

Topic of Book

Key Points

Chapter 1	Chapter 2	Chapter 3

Chapter 4	Chapter 5	Chapter 6

Anything's Possible

Name _____ Date _____

Hyperlinking through the Solar System
Genres Chart

Reality (fact)	Fantasy (fiction)

Name _____ Date _____

Seven Wonders of the World
Timeline

Year	Name of "Wonder"
1.	
2.	
3.	
4.	
5.	
6.	
7.	
8.	
9.	
10.	
11.	
12.	
13.	
14.	

Name _____ Date _____

Race to Space
Sequencing Chart

List steps or events in time order (in the order they occurred in the story).

Topic:
First:
Next:
Next:
Next:
Next:
Next:
Next:
Finally:

Name _____ Date _____

Around the World
Book Report Form

List the key points from the book you read.

Topic of Book

Key Points

Chapter 1

Chapter 2

Chapter 3

Chapter 4

Chapter 5

Chapter 6

Name _____ Date _____

Earth Belongs to You
Content Web

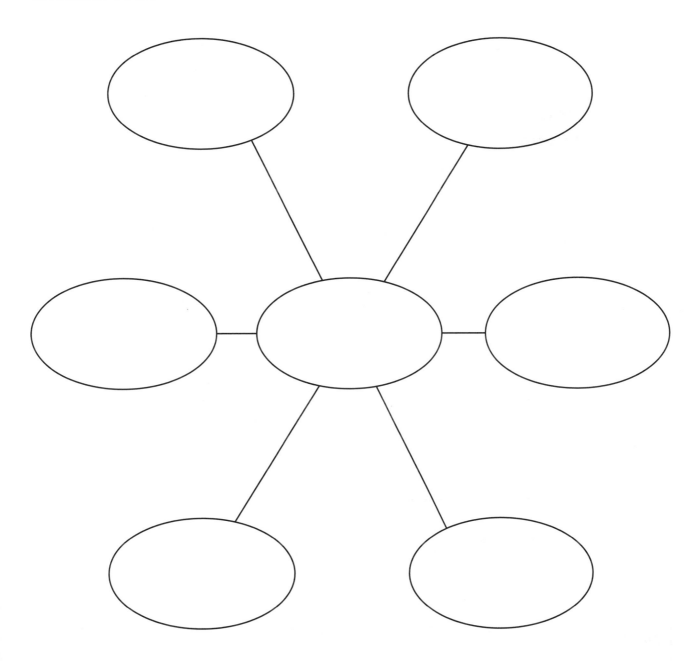

Name _____ Date _____

Treasure Island
Story Grammar Map

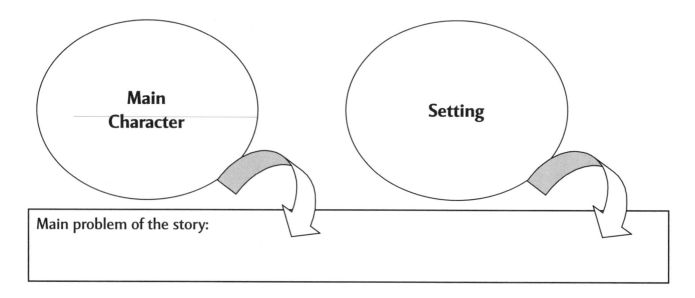

Main Character

Setting

Main problem of the story:

An event in the story:

An event in the story:

How was the story's problem solved?

What is the ending?

Name _____ Date _____

Gulliver's Travels
Compare and Contrast Chart

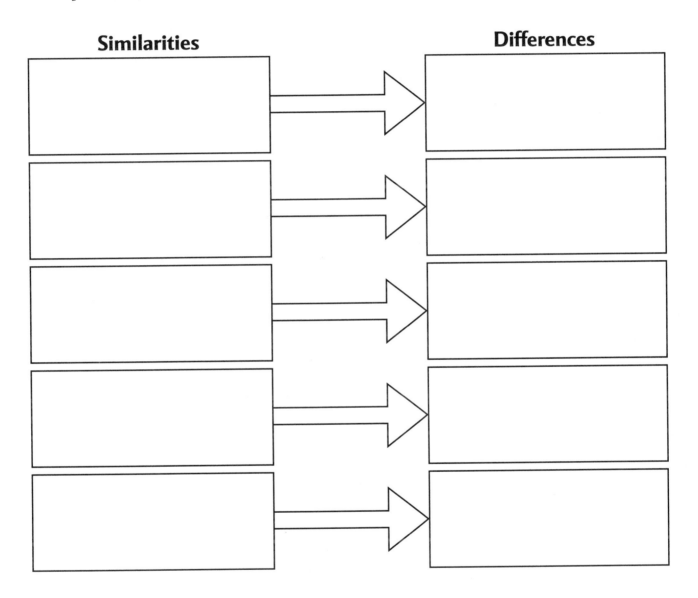

Similarities   **Differences**